D1295924

Framing Democracy

Framing Democracy

A BEHAVIORAL APPROACH TO DEMOCRATIC THEORY

Jamie Terence Kelly

PRINCETON UNIVERSITY PRESS
PRINCETON AND OXFORD

ISBN 978-0-691-15519-7

Library of Congress Control Number: 2012941111

British Library Cataloging-in-Publication Data is available

This book has been composed in Sabon

Printed on acid-free paper. ∞

Printed in the United States of America

10 9 8 7 6 5 4 3 2 1

For Mia

Contents

Acknowledgments

THIS PROJECT has been a long time in the making, and so there are a great many people who deserve my gratitude, not all of whom can be listed here. As in all things, I must begin by thanking Marie and Josephine, my parents Jim and Lucia, and my sister Cassandra.

Reflecting back on the path that took me here, I realize how much my experiences—first as an undergraduate and then as a M.A. student—in Carleton University's philosophy department have shaped the way I think and write. In particular, I would like to thank professors Andrew Brook, Marvin Glass, Rebecca Kukla, and Richard Manning. With specific regard to this project, I realize now that conversations, arguments, and courses with students from the Institute of Cognitive Science have structured the way I think about empirical research and philosophical argumentation. I received a better philosophical education at Carleton University than I deserved, and for that I will always be grateful.

At Boston University, I was fortunate to find the guidance and tutelage of professors Hugh Baxter, David Lyons, Juliet Floyd, and David Roochnik, among others. In graduate school, one seems to learn as much from one's peers as from one's professors, and so I must thank all of my colleagues at BU for their support, friendship, insight, and encouragement. In particular, I wouldn't be who I am today without Timothy Brownlee, David Jennings, Anthony Reeves, and Matthew Schaffer. Further, I owe a huge intellectual debt to David Estlund of Brown University. His work has shaped the way I think about democracy, and his advice was invaluable in forming the arguments (at least the good ones) of this book.

Since my arrival in 2008, Vassar College has been enormously supportive of my research. Barry Lam provided me with important feedback and guidance on my manuscript. Maria Höhn was instrumental in steering the project to completion. The dean of the faculty, Jonathan Chenette, has been supportive at every turn, and the research committee has been unfailingly helpful. I would also like to thank all the students who participated in my seminars on Theories of Democracy in the spring semesters of 2009 and 2011. For their assistance with the manuscript, I thank Matthew Bishop, Benjamin Conant, Hannah Groch-Begley, and Julia Nethero.

For their insight and criticisms, I am grateful to the two anonymous reviewers for Princeton University Press. I also thank Rob Tempio and the whole editorial team at the press.

Finally, I am grateful for financial support provided by the Ontario Graduate Scholarship Program, the Social Sciences and Humanities Research Council of Canada, the Helen G. Allen Award from the Boston University Center for the Humanities, the H. B. Earhart Foundation, and the Elinor Nims Brink fund at Vassar College.

Introduction

BEHAVIORAL LAW AND ECONOMICS grew out of the larger disciplines of economics and legal theory as a result of a desire to incorporate insights from empirical psychology into theorizing about markets and the law.[1] These subdisciplines reject the rational actor model of human decision making (often referred to as *homo economicus*[2]) and replace it with a picture of humans as boundedly rational, where the bounds of our rationality are drawn by heuristics that, under certain specifiable conditions, result in biases in our choices. These two disciplines have generated important insights into how certain facts about human decision making affect our behavior both in markets and in legal settings. In this book I argue that, just as in economics and law, normative democratic theory must begin to pay attention to the picture of human choice described by empirical psychology. Thus, I develop a behavioral approach to normative democratic theory.[3]

There are of course important differences between economics, law, and democratic theory. Unlike democratic theory, economics and (to a lesser degree) law have important descriptive components. That is, both

[1] For a broad statement of this approach to law, see the work of Sunstein, Jolls, and Thaler (Sunstein 1997; Jolls, Sunstein, et al. 1998; Jolls 2006). For compilations of articles on this topic, see Sunstein (2000a), Parisi and Smith (2005), and the Vanderbilt Law Review Symposium on the subject (Hurd et al. 1998). For skepticism about this approach, see Posner (1998), Rostain (2000), and Mitchell (2002a, 2002b).

For a popular and accessible introduction to behavioral economics, see Ariely (2009). For more technical descriptions, see Camerer (1999, 2003) and Camerer, Loewenstein, and Rabin (2003). For a critical perspective on behavioral economics, see the work of Gerd Gigerenzer (2008) and Nathan Berg (Berg and Gigerenzer 2010).

[2] For a helpful discussion of this term, see Thaler (2000a).

[3] I should note that the behavioral approach I propose here is, despite some superficial similarities, importantly distinct from forms of behaviorism. In general, behaviorism was a movement in psychology and philosophy characterized by an aversion to the use of psychological or mental states in scientific (Skinner 1953) or philosophical inquiry (Quine 1960). A behaviorist was thus someone who greatly preferred behavioral evidence to autobiographical reports regarding internal states (Sellars 1963). The behavioral approach developed here shares an emphasis on the methodological importance of behavior, but it has no particular skepticism about internal mental states. The behavioral sciences to which I make reference object to the use of empirically unsupported hypotheses about human behavior, but they commonly rely on first-person reports regarding mental states (Tversky and Kahneman 1982). As a result, the behavioral approach developed here should not be confused with behaviorism. In what follows I will use the terms "behavioral approach to democratic theory" and "behavioral democratic theory" roughly interchangeably.

attempt to accurately describe human decision making in certain contexts. Thus, for law and economics, incorporating insights from psychology was important simply to enable them to provide a more accurate description of economic and legal decision making. It would be wrong, however, to claim that either economics or law is focused exclusively on descriptions. To the contrary, many economists and legal theorists are concerned with improving our institutions, policies, and decisions. This normative orientation is clear in the case of behavioral law and economics, where efforts to debias decision making have moved to the forefront of theoretical debates.[4]

Still, it should be noted that democratic theory is, when compared with other theoretical enterprises, a distinctively normative affair (I will not here concern myself with merely descriptive accounts of democracy). As a result, the motivation to develop a behavioral approach to democratic theory cannot be premised merely on a desire to provide a more accurate description of democratic decisions. Descriptions of this sort are quite alien to democratic theorists, especially those of a philosophical bent. Instead, looking to psychology and other social sciences for insight into human behavior must be understood as being geared toward achieving democratic theory's normative goals. Behavioral democratic theory must be interested in bounded rationality as means to arrive at a better understanding of the moral consequences of democratic government.[5]

This, however, is where things get complicated. The notion of a unified enterprise of "democratic theory" is but a useful conceit. In truth, there is no one democratic theory but rather a huge proliferation of theories of democracy. As a result, understanding the moral implications of a behavioral approach to democratic theory will require us to consider a wide range of theories of democracy and show how the rejection of the rational actor model affects each of them. Further, the implications of adopting a picture of humans as boundedly rational depend heavily on which bounds we consider. There is currently much controversy regarding how best to understand the heuristics that characterize human decisions and regarding which ones ought to count as biases. As a result, the

---

[4] See Jolls and Sunstein's "Debiasing through Law" (2006).

[5] Although some might construe the evidence I consider as providing reasons to reject democracy altogether (in favor of some nondemocratic alternative), I choose here to investigate whether empirical research can help us to understand and evaluate different theories of democracy. One of the interesting things about political philosophy in the past seventy-five years is that the greatest controversy is no longer between democratic and nondemocratic forms of government but rather between different conceptions of democracy itself. One can find within the scope of democratic theories conceptions of democracy that run the gamut from meritocratic to oligarchic, from conservative to liberal, and from capitalist to socialist. As a result, I will restrict my focus to political theories that are, at least nominally, democratic.

case for behavioral democratic theory is complicated both by the number of democratic theories and by disagreements regarding the nature of the biases that characterize human decision making.

In response to these two complications, I will narrow my focus. First, in response to the variety of extant theories of democracy, I choose to focus my attention on judgment-based theories—those that construe votes as judgments about the common good (or collective interest), rather than as individual preferences over electoral outcomes. The key difference between judgments and preferences is that judgments can be either correct or incorrect (e.g., true or false), whereas preferences are simply reports (usually taken to be veridical) about individual attitudes.[6] Thus, I will spend much of my time dealing with theories of democracy that construe democracy as an attempt to get at the truth about political matters, rather than as the interaction of brute preferences. Further, in order to organize these judgment-based theories into a manageable set, I propose a taxonomy of democratic theories that ranks them in accordance with the amount that they demand from the judgment of citizens. Preference-based theories of democracy will factor into this ranking (at the minimalist end of my ranking), but they will play a relatively minor role in the overall analysis.

Second, in response to the range of different cognitive biases that may be relevant to our understanding of democracy, I choose to focus on only one: framing effects. Very generally, a framing effect occurs when different but equivalent formulations of a problem result in substantively different decisions being made. Thus, our susceptibility to framing effects reveals that our decisions are not invariant across equivalent formulations of the same problem.[7] Although some of what I say about framing effects will apply to a more expansive appraisal of behavioral democratic theory, I will limit my conclusions here to the phenomenon of framing.[8] In order to make a convincing case for the relevance of empirical psychology to the normative study of democracy, I think it is important to be cautious. In the future I hope to generate a more expansive account of behavioral democratic theory, but in the present work I opt to take a more restricted approach. I will thus limit myself to a consideration of the well-documented failures of human decision making to live up to the rational choice principle of invariance; my aim here is to show how the

---

[6] For more on this issue, see Brennan and Pettit (1990), as well as the work of David Estlund (1990, 1994, 1995, 2008). Also, see my elaboration of the notion of judgment in section 1.5.1.

[7] I expand on this understanding of framing effects in sections 1.1.2 and 1.2.

[8] In particular, the analysis presented here may generalize to epistemic concerns regarding group polarization (Sunstein 2009a) and overconfidence bias (Griffin and Tversky 2002). However, I shall not argue for these claims here.

social scientific literature on framing effects should inform our understanding of democracy. More specifically, I will show how various theories of democracy ought to respond to framing effects. In what follows, I provide an outline of the contents of each chapter.

Chapter 1: Framing Effects. The first order of business is to introduce the phenomenon of framing. More specifically, I need to show why the fact that human decisions are not invariant over equivalent formulations of the same decision problem ought to be of any concern for political theory. In order to do this, I distinguish between two different kinds of framing effects (equivalency and emphasis), and I give reasons for thinking that emphasis framing effects will be common in politics. Further, I explain why our susceptibility to framing effects counts as a potential fetter to the reliability of democratic decisions. In very general terms, the fact that decisions are responsive to frames diminishes their ability to be responsive to good reasons. To the extent that the reliability of our decisions is dependent on our ability to be swayed by good reasons, then framing effects will negatively affect our ability to make correct decisions.

Chapter 2: Theories of Democracy. Next, in order to help organize my discussion of the panoply of extant theories of democracy, I propose a taxonomy that orients them along a spectrum of epistemic demandingness. That is, I arrange democratic theories in accordance with how much each theory demands of citizens' judgment in order to secure the goods democracy is taken to offer. In this chapter I allow theories of democracy to specify their own epistemic demands, without challenging their claims regarding how much they actually require from the judgment of citizens. My aim here is exegetical; I postpone my critical analysis of these theories until chapter 4.

Chapter 3: Behavioral Democratic Theory. In this chapter, I argue that a behavioral approach to democratic theory has a number of distinct advantages over other approaches. In particular, I contrast a behavioral approach with three more common ways of treating the decision making of citizens in a democracy. For the sake of simplicity, I use the notion of epistemic competence to stand in for the various cognitive skills and abilities that are required for democracy to function properly.

Unlike the other approaches I consider, a behavioral approach to democratic theory provides us with a way to reconcile normative claims about democracy with troubling empirical evidence regarding the epistemic abilities of citizens. Behavioral democratic theory can do so by assessing the benefits of attaining the standard of competence required by a given theory of democracy and comparing these benefits to the likely costs of bringing our current epistemic abilities into line with that standard. By construing competence in terms of the relative costs and benefits of achieving and maintaining a competent citizenry, it is possible to propose and evaluate reforms for democratic institutions that are capable of augmenting the epistemic reliability of democratic decision making. In order to do so, however, behavioral democratic theory must rely on descriptions of the state of our epistemic capacities provided by psychology and other social sciences. As a result, a behavioral approach to democratic theory must reject idealized pictures of human decision making and begin to consider how cognitive pathologies such as framing effects ought to affect our understanding of democratic arrangements.

Chapter 4: Behavioral Democratic Theory Applied. In this chapter, I apply the behavioral approach to particular theories of democracy. More specifically, I show how the phenomenon of framing effects is relevant to the normative theories of democracy presented in chapter 2. I hope to generate two results here that will validate the behavioral approach. The first concerns democratic theories at the minimalist end of my spectrum. The second result applies to theories of democracy that place epistemic demands on the judgment of citizens.

First, I attempt to demonstrate that minimalist theories of democracy (those that require little, if anything from the judgment of citizens) can generate only weak moral reasons for endorsing democratic government. Most such theories are unaffected by my concerns regarding framing effects. I here point out, however, just how thin the normative justifications of these theories have to be in order for them to be entitled to ignore concerns like framing. Purely procedural theories of democracy can ignore framing effects only insofar as they deny that we can expect democracies to make good political decisions. This results in a very thin procedural endorsement of democratic government. On closer inspection, however, many forms of pure proceduralism turn out not to be so pure after all. Fairness theories and deep deliberative theories often rely on hidden epistemic claims about the reliability of democratic decisions. As a consequence, however, impure proceduralisms are obliged to give up their status as minimalist theories of democracy.

The second result I hope to generate in this chapter concerns theories closer to the epistemic end of my spectrum. I argue that theories of democracy that place epistemic demands on the judgment of citizens must account for the costs of ensuring that this judgment is accurate. In this way, any theory of democracy that purports to give us epistemic reasons to support democratic institutions should be obliged to account for how this epistemic value is to be secured. As a result, I argue that such theories ought to endorse institutional mechanisms capable of bolstering citizens' judgment.

Chapter 5: Institutional Implications.   If the arguments in the previous chapters are successful, then framing effects pose a threat to the epistemic value of democratic government. Further, a behavioral approach to democratic theory requires us to incorporate into our favored normative theory arguments for the feasibility of achieving competence. The big question for the last chapter is: How can an even moderately epistemic theory argue for the epistemic value of democracy if individual decision making is susceptible to framing effects? My answer is to point to a number of plausible institutional reforms that could help to secure the epistemic value of democratic decision making even in the face of framing.

In order to counteract the effects of framing, three broad strategies suggest themselves. First, increasing the number of competing frames for political issues (e.g., by ensuring a diversity of political and media perspectives) holds out the possibility of making us more responsive to reasons than to frames. Second, mechanisms designed to isolate democratic outcomes from flawed democratic decision making (e.g., constitutional review) might allow us to catch mistakes before they undermine the epistemic value of democratic arrangements. Third, public education programs aimed at eliminating framing effects could provide us with a direct means of improving the decision making of democracies.

My discussion of these issues is only preliminary. The point of this chapter is to sketch the resources that theories of democracy have at their disposal to vindicate their claims about the purported epistemic value of democratic arrangements. I do not attempt here to make the case in favor of the feasibility of epistemic theories of democracy; I merely indicate the kind of work that needs to be done in order to reconcile the normative claims of such theories with the empirical literature on framing effects. Individual theories will have to make different arguments and put forward different institutional proposals in order to show how citizens are to live up to their epistemic obligations (e.g., fairness theories may well be satisfied with a system of judicial review, but theories of democracy that make use of Condorcet's jury theorem seem to require a broad reform of current systems of political communication). My aim in this chapter is not to make the argument for these theories but only to show that behavioral democratic theory can respond to questions about the reliability of democratic decision making. Whether these responses are ultimately satisfying is another matter, one that I cannot address here, but I hope to have shown that democratic theory should no longer remain silent on these questions.

CHAPTER ONE

Framing Effects

1.1 THE BEHAVIORAL APPROACH

Recently, the behavioral approach to law (Sunstein and Thaler 2008), economics (Ariely 2009), and other social sciences (Shleifer 2000; Shefrin 2002) has been gaining popularity.[1] This approach is characterized by an attempt to reform existing disciplines (e.g., law, economics, and finance) through the development of a new model of human decision making (H. Simon 1955; Gintis 2004). Traditionally, these disciplines have employed a model of choice borrowed from classical economics.[2] This model construes individuals as maximally rational and seeks to understand human behavior in terms of a set of optimal rules for the solution of decision-making problems. This approach has been criticized on a number of levels (Jolls, Sunstein, et al. 1998), but most important for my purposes, it has long been shown to present an inaccurate description of actual human decisions (Kahneman, Slovic, et al. 1982; Kahneman 2003).

The behavioral approach to law and economics (as well as other disciplines) arose out of an attempt to develop an account of human decision making that more accurately reflects our actual decision-making behavior. In order to do so, this approach incorporates insights from empirical psychology into theorizing about markets and the law. The behavioral subdisciplines of economics and law reject the traditional rational actor model of human decision making and attempt to generate a new, behavioral model of choice. The picture of human decision making that has emerged from these subdisciplines construes human beings as boundedly rational, where the bounds of our rationality are drawn by cognitive heuristics that, under certain specifiable conditions, result in biases in our decision making.[3] So far, the behavioral approach has proved to be highly

---

[1] The term "behavioral law" is potentially misleading. Originally, most behavioral research in legal theory concerned the law and economics paradigm. As a result, this research was normally understood as "behavioral law and economics." Recently, however, the behavioral approach has been applied to new areas of law and legal scholarship (Sunstein 1993b; Jolls and Sunstein 2006). For the sake of simplicity, I will refer to this literature as behavioral law.

[2] The logical foundations of this approach can be traced back to the early game-theoretical analyses of Von Neumann and Morgenstern (1944).

[3] In these contexts, a heuristic is a simple, easily applied rule for solving decision problems. These shortcuts normally provide a reliable means for solving complex problems but sometimes lead to poor decisions (Gilovich et al. 2002).

productive, generating important insights into how certain facts about the decision making of humans affects our behavior both in markets and in legal settings.[4]

1.1.1 Heuristics and Biases

The behavioral approach to both law and economics has drawn heavily on an empirical literature started by psychologists Daniel Kahneman and Amos Tversky.[5] Since the 1970s, Kahneman and Tversky have studied the effect of risk and uncertainty on human decision making.[6] This psychological research, commonly known as the "heuristics and biases" literature, has become highly influential in economics,[7] law,[8] and political science.[9]

The heuristics and biases literature represents a rejection of the rational actor model of human decision making in that it purports to show that human decisions do not operate on the basis of the rules outlined by rational choice theory. Instead, Kahneman and Tversky have argued that we rely on a small set of relatively efficient, low-information, cognitive shortcuts to solve decision problems. These heuristics do not conform to the requirements of rational choice theory, and thus this literature has helped to explain why, in so many different contexts, actual human decisions fail to be fully rational. In this way, the heuristics and biases

---

[4] For an interesting example, see behavioral law and economics' treatment of the endowment effect, the Coase theorem, and environmental law (Sunstein 1993b; Jolls and Sunstein 2006). For a broad overview of how these heuristics and biases impact on public policy, see Trout (2009).

[5] It should be noted at the outset that the relationship between the behavioral approach and the heuristics and biases research is contingent: this approach seeks to improve on the rational actor model by looking to empirical psychology, and currently the most important research on choice in psychology is the heuristics and biases literature. If this literature is supplanted or discredited by another research project, then the behavioral approach should seek other empirical grounds for its model of choice. Currently, however, the research project started by Kahneman and Tversky is the most promising behavioral model of choice.

[6] Amos Tversky died in 1996. He was professor of behavioral sciences at Stanford University. Daniel Kahneman won the 2002 Bank of Sweden Prize in Economic Sciences for their research. He is currently emeritus professor of psychology and public affairs at Princeton University. Major contributions to this field of research have been compiled in three volumes: *Judgment under Uncertainty* (Kahneman, Slovic, et al. 1982), *Choices, Values, and Frames* (Kahneman and Tversky 2000c), and *Heuristics and Biases* (Gilovich et al. 2002).

[7] See *Quasi Rational Economics* (Thaler 1991) and *Advances in Behavioral Economics* (Camerer, Loewenstein, et al. 2003).

[8] See *Behavioral Law and Economics* (Sunstein 2000a) and *The Law and Economics of Irrational Behavior* (Parisi and Smith 2005).

[9] See *Elements of Reason* (Lupia et al. 2000).

literature presents an alternative model of human decision making: the heuristics specified by this literature can be used as a behavioral model for the study of human decisions. The predictions of this behavioral model differ significantly in many (though not all) situations from those of the rational actor model.[10]

In recent years there has been a huge proliferation of research into behavioral models of human decision making.[11] A large number of individual heuristics and biases have been studied, and there is much controversy regarding the proper way to characterize many of these phenomena.[12] As a result, much of the empirical literature on behavioral models of choice is still under development.[13] Because the literature has become so vast, and so much of it remains controversial, it is not yet possible to speak conclusively about a single, unified, and complete behavioral model of choice. Instead, such a model now exists only in bits and pieces, with varying degrees of controversy and empirical disagreement attached to each. As a result of the current instability of the wider behavioral research program, in what follows, I will focus on just one well-documented aspect of the heuristics and biases literature: the phenomenon of framing effects.

1.1.2 Framing Effects

An influential part of the heuristics and biases project involves the study of how experimental subjects respond to decisions involving risk.[14] Kahneman and Tversky have attempted to provide a general account of the heuristics that determine in which situations individuals will display risk-averse and risk-seeking behavior.[15] As part of this project, they conducted experiments to show how the wording of a decision problem served to influence the responses they received from experimental subjects. The

[10] For a litany of interesting examples, see the work of Richard Thaler (esp. 1991, 1992, 2005).

[11] For accessible introductions to this literature, see Gilovich (1991), Piattelli-Palmarini (1994), Sunstein and Thaler (2008), and Ariely (2009).

[12] For a sustained critique of this literature, see the work of Gerd Gigerenzer (Gigerenzer, Todd, et al. 1999; Gigerenzer and Selten 2001; Gigerenzer and Engel 2006; Gigerenzer 2008; Berg and Gigerezer 2010).

[13] Kahneman and Tversky's prospect theory continues to be the most dominant paradigm in the field (Camerer 2000; Kahneman and Tversky 2000a, 2000d), but other versions (Wakker and Tversky 1993) and alternatives (Loomes and Sugden 1982) also exist.

[14] Also instrumental to the development of research into framing effects was work by sociologists such as William Gamson. See especially Gamson (1992), as well as Gamson and Modigliani (1987, 1989).

[15] See "Choices, Values, and Frames" and "Prospect Theory: An Analysis of Decision under Risk" in Kahneman and Tversky (2000c).

result was the first systematic empirical examination of framing effects. The most widely cited example from their research continues to be their "Asian disease problem."[16]

The Asian disease

Imagine that the United States is preparing for the outbreak of an unusual Asian disease, which is expected to kill 600 people. Two alternative programs to combat the disease have been proposed. Assume that the exact scientific estimates of the consequences of the programs are as follows:

If Program A is adopted, 200 people will be saved

If Program B is adopted, there is a one-third probability that 600 people will be saved and a two-thirds probability that no people will be saved

In this version of the problem, a substantial majority of respondents favor Program A, indicating risk aversion. Other respondents, selected at random, receive a question in which the same cover story is followed by a different description of the options:

If Program A' is adopted, 400 people will die

If Program B' is adopted, there is a one-third probability that nobody will die and a two-thirds probability that 600 people will die

A substantial majority of respondents now favor Program B', the risk-seeking option. Although there is no substantive difference between the versions, they evoke different associations and evaluations. (Kahneman 2003, 1458)

Here, Program A and Program A' are equivalent (200 people saved; 400 people dead) and Program B and Program B' are equivalent (one-third probability of 600 people saved; two-thirds probability of 600 dead), while A and A' (the risk-averse options) are different from B and B' (the risk-seeking options).[17] The manner in which these outcomes are framed, however, causes respondents to express contrary preferences (i.e., the certain outcome is more popular when the decision is framed in terms of saving people, whereas the risky outcome is more popular when the

---

[16] Originally published in "The Framing of Decisions and the Psychology of Choice" (Kahneman and Tversky 1981).

[17] It should be noted, however, that in both versions of the problem, the two options have the same expected value (i.e., $1/3 \times 600 = 200$ and $2/3 \times 600 = 400$). Kahneman and Tversky designed the example so as to highlight how the framing of a decision can influence our choice of a risk-averse or risk-seeking option (Druckman and McDermott 2008, 305).

decision is framed in terms of avoiding death). This serves as evidence for the conclusion that the description of a problem scenario can significantly affect the judgments and preferences of subjects. This is the case despite the fact that the different descriptions are, and can easily be recognized to be, equivalent.

1.1.3 Invariance

Kahneman and Tversky have presented the results of the Asian disease problem and other experiments as a challenge to rational choice theory's principle of invariance:

> Invariance requires that the preference order between prospects should not depend on the manner in which they are described. In particular, two versions of a choice problem that are recognized to be equivalent when shown together should elicit the same preference even when shown separately. We now show that the requirement of invariance, however elementary and innocuous it may seem, cannot generally be satisfied. (Kahneman and Tversky 2000b, 4)

The principle of invariance (referred to by Kenneth Arrow as the principle of extensionality[18]) requires that rational decisions must be invariant across equivalent formulations of the same problem. This principle forms a core part of the rational actor model of human decision making traditionally relied on in economics and related disciplines. It requires that individuals ignore arbitrary changes to the presentation of a choice scenario and focus only on outcomes. If individuals make different decisions when presented with different formulations of the same decision problem, then they fail to satisfy what Arrow called a "fundamental element of rationality, so elementary that we hardly notice it" (Arrow 1982, 6). Kahneman and Tversky, for their part, claim that the "moral of these results is disturbing: Invariance is normatively essential, intuitively compelling, and psychologically unfeasible" (Kahneman and Tversky 2000b, 6).

Abandoning the principle of invariance leads to a model of choice that predicts that individuals will respond in different ways to a given decision problem, depending on how it is framed. It should be emphasized that abandoning the principle of invariance does not entail that human decisions will be chaotic, random, or ultimately unpredictable. Instead, the central insight of Kahneman and Tversky's work was that framing a risky choice in terms of losses or gains would have a predictable effect on individual decisions (i.e., certain kinds of frames lead individuals to make

[18] See "Risk Perception in Psychology and Economics" (Arrow 1982).

risk-averse decisions, while other frames lead them to be risk-seeking). Human decision making, despite its quirks, appears to result from the interaction of a number of relatively simple, discernible rules. Although there is still disagreement about the specific nature of these behavioral rules, empirical research has for some time now shown that the framing of decisions reliably affects human decision making. As a result, the empirical study of framing effects has become a mainstay of behavioral research in economics, law, and related social sciences.

1.2 Research on Framing

Given the massive amount of existing research, I will not attempt to describe all the empirical complexities of the social scientific literature on framing effects. Instead, I will provide a quick sketch of some of the most important studies and attempt to explain how they are relevant to the normative study of politics. In particular, I will be concerned to show how rejecting the principle of invariance results in a more plausible model of human decision making. In later chapters I will demonstrate how acknowledging our susceptibility to framing effects leads to specific conclusions about the design of public institutions in a democracy. For now, however, I am concerned with adequately describing the phenomena in question.[19]

1.2.1 Equivalency Framing Effects

Initially, the manner in which Kahneman and Tversky defined the phenomenon of framing effects was conservative.[20] In their seminal studies, they restricted framing effects to cases in which alternative presentations (the frames) of the decision problem were equivalent and recognized by the respondents as such. Thus, it was only because the experimental subjects in the Asian disease study would assent to the fact that Program A was equivalent to Program A′ and that Program B was equivalent to Program B′ that Kahneman and Tversky were willing to attribute the divergence in choices to the effects of framing (Kahneman 2002, 457). Let us define this kind of phenomenon as an equivalency framing effect: *An equivalency framing effect occurs when different but formally equivalent presentations of a decision problem elicit different choices.*

---

[19] In the following sections, I have adapted the distinction between equivalency and emphasis framing effects from the work of James Druckman. In particular, see "The Implications of Framing Effects for Citizen Competence" (Druckman 2001b).

[20] In particular, see their Asian disease problem (above).

More recently (especially in economics), the study of framing effects has been expanded to cases in which researchers can prove the values to be equivalent, even if the experimental subjects do not themselves recognize this. For example, even if subjects did not readily see that Programs B and B′ were equivalent, we could demonstrate their equivalence by uncontroversial mathematical means. In order to retain this conservative definition of framing, the study of framing effects had to focus on situations involving quantifiable values. Here, it is easy to demonstrate equivalence when dealing with things like lottery payoffs, probability calculations, and outcome statistics for medical treatments.[21]

For an example, take the case of an influential study conducted in 1982 by a group of researchers investigating the possibility that framing effects might impact the decision making of patients in health-care scenarios. In this study, the researchers tried to determine whether framing outcome statistics for cancer treatment in terms of survival rates or mortality rates would influence individual choices. Posing a hypothetical choice scenario, they gave subjects the option of pursuing either surgery or radiation treatment for lung cancer. They then monitored the respondents' choices in order to determine whether the manner in which the outcome statistics were presented would have any effect on the rate at which each option was chosen:

> We presented a large number of outpatients, physicians, and graduate students with information describing the possible outcomes of two alternative therapies for lung cancer. The respondents appeared to comprehend and use these data. An interview with the patients after the experiment indicated that they understood the data and were able to recall important items of information. However, the choices of both naive subjects (patients) and sophisticated subjects (physicians) were influenced by several variations in the nature of the data and the form in which they were presented. (McNeil et al. 1982, 392)
>
> Perhaps our most notable finding is the effect on people's choices of presenting the data in terms of survival or death. Surgery appeared to be much more attractive when the outcomes where framed in terms of the probability of survival rather than in terms of the probability of death. We attribute this result to the fact that the risk of perioperative death looms larger when it is presented in terms of mortality than when it is presented in terms of survival. Unlike the preceding effects, which can be justified or at least rationalized, this effect of using different terminology to describe outcome represents a cognitive illusion. The effect observed in this study is large (25 percent vs. 42 percent) and

[21] These examples refer to "Rational Choice and the Framing of Decisions," Kahneman and Tversky (1986).

consistent: It holds for both cumulative-probability and life-expectancy data, for both identified and unidentified treatments, and for all three populations of subjects. Much to our surprise, the effect was not generally smaller for the physicians (who had considerable experience in evaluating medical data) or for graduate students (who had received statistical training) than for the patients (who had neither). (McNeil et al. 1982, 392–393)[22]

In cases such as these it is a simple matter to demonstrate that a 90 percent short-term survival rate is equivalent to a 10 percent immediate mortality rate. As a result, the fact that individuals respond differently to the choice between radiation treatment and surgery (depending on whether the decision is framed in terms of the probability of living or the probability of dying) can be attributed to the efficacy of framing.

1.2.2 Emphasis Framing Effects

There are many instances, however, where there exist no reliable means of demonstrating equivalence but where framing still seems to occur. Let us define this kind of phenomenon as an emphasis framing effect: *An emphasis framing effect occurs when emphasizing different elements of a decision problem elicits different choices.* These cases are more problematic than equivalency framing effects because, in any given instance, it is possible to claim that the different frames in fact represent different choices. Given that there are no means of demonstrating their formal equivalence, many experimental subjects will not assent to the frames being equivalent, providing instead some explanation of how the frames differ.[23] This results in a problem. If, in any purported case of framing, we cannot demonstrate that the frames are equivalent, then how can we be sure that emphasis framing effects ever occur? Here is another way of presenting this problem: perhaps emphasizing different elements of a decision problem in fact always produces different decisions.

A number of things can be said here. First, there is an inductive argument to be made for the existence of emphasis framing effects. Second, there is an intuitive case for framing in these situations. Third, we must realize that it is not imperative that we arrive at a consensus that any

---

[22] Similar results have been reported since this early study (Redelmeier, Rozin, et al. 1993; Redelmeier and Shafir 1995; Bernstein et al. 1999; Wills 1999; Edwards et al. 2001; Armstrong et al. 2002). For an anthology of articles on decision making in health care, see *Decision Making in Health Care* (Chapman and Sonnenberg 2000). For an account of the relationship between informed consent and framing, see "Informed Consent and the Construction of Values" (MacLean 2006).

[23] This often occurs even with equivalency framing effects. See "Reasons for Framing Effects" (Frisch 1993).

individual purported instance of framing really represents a framing effect, but only that we show that framing effects do occur in many instances.

We should note that in domains where the demonstrability condition is met (such as those studied in psychology, economics, and related social sciences), framing effects appear regularly.[24] Equivalency framing effects have been documented in situations as diverse as personal finance (Kahneman, Knetsch, et al. 2000a), the labor supply of taxi drivers (Camerer, Babcock, et al. 2000), the choice of medical treatments (McNeil et al. 1982), jury deliberations (McCaffery et al. 2002), and consumer choices regarding ground beef (Levin and Gaeth 1988). These examples all involve at least three things: uncertainty, risk, and quantifiable values. Emphasis framing effects, should they exist, would involve only the first two: uncertainty and risk. There is, however, no reason that to think that our susceptibility to frames extends only to domains in which there exist quantifiable values. Therefore, given the pervasiveness of frames in those areas in which we can verify their existence through formal proofs, I think we are entitled to expect the efficacy of framing in other areas as well.

This inference is not so bald as it might seem. That two alternative presentations of a decision problem are substantially the same, even if not formally equivalent, can often be observed quite readily. In what follows, I will provide a series of examples in which emphasis framing effects have been studied, and I hope these will suffice to show that even when the demonstrability condition is not satisfied, framing effects clearly occur.

Finally, I should point out that I do not need to insist that any two particular descriptions of a choice scenario are qualitatively identical. In the absence of the ability to demonstrate equivalence, there will be disagreement about particular cases, but that is not devastating to my argument. All I want to show is that emphasis framing effects do exist, and that they exist in numbers and in ways that ought to be of political concern.

For the reasons stated above, emphasis framing effects represent a more complicated and more interesting category of framing than equivalency framing effects. Emphasis framing effects are more complicated because they will always involve some amount of controversy, but they are more interesting because they involve scenarios that are more obviously politically salient. Although it is surely the case that in some instances (such as referendums on tax initiatives, or in debates regarding the public expenditure of specific sums) equivalency framing effects will be evident,[25]

---

[24] See, for example, "The Influence of Framing on Risky Decisions: A Meta-Analysis" (Kühberger 1998). For a critical assessment of the literature, see "All Frames are Not Created Equal" (Levin, Schneider, et al. 1998).

[25] For a study of some related cases in legal settings, see "Economic Preferences or Attitude Expressions? An Analysis of Dollar Responses to Public Issues" (Kahneman, Ritov, et

framing effects, where they occur in political settings, will normally lack the sort of easy demonstrability that is characteristic of equivalency framing effects. As a result, studies of emphasis framing effects should be of particular concern to political philosophers.

In the past, there have been a number of ways in which these sorts of effects have been studied in the social sciences. Failures to respect the principle of invariance had been the subject of study long before Kahneman and Tversky popularized the term "framing effect," and in the following sections I describe some of the various guises under which they have been described and introduce some current research as well.

1.2.2.1 QUESTION-ORDERING EFFECTS

In 1980, Howard Schuman and Stuart Presser[26] replicated a famous Cold War question-ordering experiment concerning communist reporters. This experiment, originally conducted by Herbert Hyman and Paul Sheatsley thirty years earlier,[27] reveals that failures of invariance can be induced by changing the order in which questions are posed to experimental subjects. In both sets of experiments, subjects were asked a number of questions with the following two items mixed in:

> *Communist reporter item:* Do you think the United States should let Communist reporters from other countries come in here and send back to their papers the news as they see it?
> *American reporter item:* Do you think a Communist country like Russia should let American newspaper reporters come in and send back to America the news as they see it? (Schuman, Kalton, et al. 1983, 112–113)

The experimenters found that when they asked the American reporter question first, followed by the communist reporter question, respondents were far more likely to advocate granting access to communists than when they introduced the items in the reverse order. Similarly, respondents were far less likely to expect that American reporters should be granted access when the communist reporter question was asked first, followed by the American reporter question. As Schuman and Presser point out, when the American reporter item is introduced first, it encourages respondents to consider a norm of reciprocity in addressing the question about communist reporters. Similarly, when the communist reporter item is introduced

---

al. 2000) and "Predictably Incoherent Judgments" (Sunstein, Kahneman, et al. 2002).

[26] See *Questions and Answers in Attitude Surveys* (Schuman and Presser 1981).

[27] "The Current Status of American Public Opinion" (Hyman and Sheatsley 1950).

first, respondents are inclined to show consistency in their response to the American reporter question.[28]

In this example, we can see both the controversy and the import of emphasis framing effects. The example is controversial because the question order seems to introduce different normative considerations into the subjects' decision making. As a result, one might claim that the questions are in fact not equivalent. These kinds of examples are interesting, however, because political issues are often presented in groups, and their ordering is subject to variation and manipulation. As a result, question-ordering effects of the sort above seem particularly relevant to our thinking about contemporary politics.

1.2.2.2 QUESTION-WORDING EFFECTS

Social scientists who study survey responses have long had a wealth of data drawn from the U.S. General Social Survey. Since it began in 1972, this survey has kept an account of American responses to a wide range of social and policy concerns. Beginning in the 1980s, its creators began varying the wording of selected questions in order to explore the effect of word-choice on survey responses. Since then, a number of researchers have been mining this data to determine what effect the choice of wording has on individuals' responses to questions about public policies.[29]

In 1984, Kenneth Rasinski began evaluating the effect of these variations on the perception of issues concerning different kinds of government spending. He monitored how subtle changes in the language used to describe federal programs during the years 1984, 1985, and 1986 affected the responses of survey respondents. For example, he found that "[r]esults for all three years show that greater support was found for 'solving the problem of big cities' than for 'assistance to big cities.' Similarly, more support was found for 'improving the conditions of blacks' than for 'assistance to blacks'" (Rasinski 1989, 392). Rasinski monitored the wording of questions concerning government programs in many different spheres, including space exploration, the environment, health, assistance to cities, law enforcement, drug rehabilitation, education, assistance to African Americans, the military, foreign aid, and welfare (390). He found that "[t]he question wording experiments show that issue labeling and enhancement can have a substantial effect on public support for some

---

[28] For an interesting and very sophisticated analysis of the instability of survey responses, see Dean Lacy's work on nonseparable preferences (2001a and 2001b).

[29] See "The Effect of Question Wording on Public Support for Government Spending" (Rasinski 1989); "Framing Responsibility for Political Issues: The Case of Poverty" (Iyengar 1990); "That Which We Call Welfare by Any Other Name Would Smell Sweeter" (T. Smith 1987).

issues. The effect of labeling was quite robust, showing similar effects within the three years" (392).

And as Larry Bartels points out (somewhat more polemically) on the basis of the same data,

> [m]ost spectacularly, while only 20–25 percent of the respondents each year said that too little was being spent on "welfare," 63–65 percent said that too little was being spent on "assistance to the poor."
>
> "Welfare" clearly has deeply unpopular connotations for significant segments of the American public and evokes rather different mental images than does "assistance to the poor." But these different images are attached to the same set of programs and policies; any effort to make subtle distinctions of substance between "welfare" and "assistance to the poor" seems fruitlessly tendentious. (Bartels 2003b, 13–14)

This research demonstrates that the language used to frame questions about public policies can have systematic effects on the responses of individuals. Changes in question wording manage to shift the emphasis onto different political considerations, thereby altering the choices of respondents. The precise nature of the psychological mechanisms operating here is disputed,[30] but the effect is clear: changing the wording of questions serves to elicit different answers from respondents. This effect is particularly striking in the above cases because the issues being queried have such obvious political importance. Other research, however, has shown that framing effects extend beyond the wording of survey questions and into more explicitly political arenas as well.

1.2.2.3 POLITICAL CONTEXT EFFECTS

Larry Bartels argues for the ubiquity and importance of framing effects in contemporary politics by presenting a number of examples of politically charged issues that appear to be susceptible to framing.[31] One of his most striking examples involves the manner in which the political context of affirmative action referendums affects the results. Bartels quotes an article titled "Houston Voters Maintain Affirmative-Action Policy" from the *New York Times*:

> In voting decisively to maintain affirmative-action policies, Houstonians…offered a window on the complicated feelings that many Americans say they have about the issue.
>
> Interviews with voters and an analysis of exit polls indicate the proposal to ban affirmative action here failed because affirmative-action

---

[30] See, for example, "Toward a Psychology of Framing Effects" (Nelson, Oxley, et al. 1997).

[31] The following example comes from "Is 'Popular Rule' Possible?" (Bartels 2003b).

supporters kept its opponents from seizing the rhetorical high ground of equal opportunity and civil rights....But the fundamental truth that seems to have emerged from the debate here is that the future of affirmative action may depend more than anything else on the language in which it is framed.

The vote Tuesday came only after a tumultuous debate in the City Council over the wording of the measure. Rather than being asked whether they wanted to ban discrimination and "preferential treatment," to which voters said a clear "yes" in California last year and to which polls showed Houston voters would also say "yes," residents were instead asked whether they wished specifically to ban affirmative action in city contracting and hiring.

The legal effect was the same under either wording, but to this revised question they answered "no," by 55 percent to 45 percent.

Affirmative-action proponents around the nation hailed not just the result of Houston's vote, but the phrasing of the referendum as a straight up-or-down call on affirmative action, and they said that is the way the question should be put to voters elsewhere.

Its opponents, meanwhile, who are already in court challenging the City Council's broad rewording as illegal, denounced it as a heavy-handed way of obscuring the principles that were really at stake. (Verhovek 1997)

This example is intended to show that public responses to pressing political issues, here affirmative action policies, are not invariant between alternative formulations of the issues in question. In the first frame, that of "banning preferential treatment," emphasis is placed on moral concerns about nondiscrimination. In the second frame, that of banning affirmative action, emphasis is placed on specific policy instruments. Once again, however, it is possible that one might take these two frames to represent altogether different choices, but that response ignores the fact that the practical outcome of the choice in either frame is identical.

Furthermore, political context effects are not limited to the manner in which the specific options are framed in referendums. The ability of media organizations and political campaigns to frame issues (independently of the formulation of the specific questions put to voters) has been the subject of a number of influential studies. For example, several experiments have shown that the manner in which affirmative action proposals are framed in the news predictably influences the amount of support the proposal will receive.[32] For instance, framing the issue in terms of

[32] See "The Changing Culture of Affirmative Action" (Gamson and Modigliani 1987); *Divided by Color* (Kinder and Sanders 1996); and "Support for a Supreme Court Affirmative Action Decision" (Clawson and Waltenburg 2003).

the preferential treatment of minorities has different effects than casting it as an effort to end racial discrimination (Clawson and Waltenburg 2003, 254).

Another example of this sort concerns citizens' responses to issues involving free speech. In recent studies, it has been shown that different media frames depicting a Ku Klux Klan rally elicit different amounts of public support.[33] Framing the issue in terms of free speech results in substantially larger amounts of support than framing it as a public safety concern:

> Two lessons may be learned from [this study]. The first is that news framing of a civil liberties confrontation matters for viewers' tolerance. Participants in this experiment, who witnessed news reports about the very same event, expressed significantly different opinions depending on media framing of that event. Those who saw a story framing the KKK rally as a free speech issue expressed greater tolerance for the Klan than did those who saw a story depicting it as a potentially explosive clash between two angry groups. The second lesson is that the effect of news frames on tolerance judgments is carried by the frames' influence on the perceived importance of specific values evoked by this issue, especially, as it turns out, the importance of maintaining public order. For framing that elevated public order concerns, tolerance was relatively lower. (Nelson, Clawson, et al. 1997, 594–595)

Here again we see that the political context used to frame an issue results in varying amounts of public support, despite the fact that the practical consequences of the policies in question remain the same.

1.3 Reception in Political Philosophy

In recent years, framing effects have been receiving increasing political and media attention.[34] They have been the subject of study in areas as diverse as the risk of AIDS (Raghubir and Menon 2001), perceptions of nanotechnology (Cobb 2005), and expansion of the European Union (Schuck and de Vreese 2006), as well as the biological bases of framing (De Martino, Kumaran, et al. 2006).[35] Now, there is of course a danger in giving too much weight to new empirical data, but the quality, amount,

---

[33] See "On the Limits of Framing Effects" (Druckman 2001c) and "Media Framing of a Civil Liberties Conflict and Its Effect on Tolerance" (Nelson, Clawson, et al. 1997).

[34] Particularly prominent is the work of George Lakoff. See, for example, *Don't Think of an Elephant!* (2004) and *The Political Mind* (2009).

[35] For more examples, see Trout (2005).

and univocacy of the empirical research here is startling. Human decisions seem to be influenced by the manner in which choices are presented. As a result, our choices often fail to respect the rational choice principle of invariance. In many situations, the frames in which choices are cast in part determine the decisions we make. This seems to be the case generally, regardless of the specific content of the decisions being made.

If the above claim is granted—that human decisions are subject to framing effects—what does it mean for political philosophy and for democratic theory in particular? In the following, I consider a number of ways in which framing effects can be construed as relevant to political philosophy. Specifically, I present and criticize three ways in which this research has recently been incorporated into democratic theory. Later (in section 1.4), I sketch a different way of integrating this information: I argue that a behavioral approach to democratic theory can use our susceptibility to framing effects to better understand the potential epistemic value of democracy and the institutions required to harness this value. For now, however, I will be concerned with how framing effects have been received by other theorists and with the shortcomings of their accounts.

1.3.1 Critique of Preference-Based Theories

One prominent way of applying framing effects to democratic theory is to view the failure of the principle of invariance as evidence for the conclusion that individuals do not have real political preferences. This view, proposed by Larry Bartels in "Democracy with Attitudes" (Bartels 2003a) is a more complex variant of a view presented much earlier by Philip Converse (Converse 1964, 1970). Bartels's most basic and influential claim is that the beliefs of citizens "are not sufficiently complete and coherent to serve as a satisfactory starting point for democratic theory, at least as it is conventionally understood" (Bartels 2003a, 49).

This claim is meant to mimic the impact of framing effects on other disciplines (especially economics) where the heuristics and biases approach has served to undermine the traditional view that individuals have purely exogenous preferences.[36] Behavioral economics (and to a growing extent behavioral law) has moved away from the claim that decision making is a straightforward matter of choosing options from an authoritative "freestanding 'preference menu'" (Sunstein 1997, 1176). Instead, it is

---

[36] Exogenous preferences (as contrasted with endogenous preferences) are fixed, stable, and independent of contextual or temporal factors. The name serves to reflect the fact that preferences of this sort originate outside the institutional, legal, and cultural context (Sunstein 1992, 295). For an anthology of articles on this subject, see *The Construction of Preference* (Lichtenstein and Slovic 2006).

acknowledged that preferences are sometimes constructed in the process of elicitation (Slovic 2000). This has led to an increased scrutiny of the manner in which choice procedures, descriptions, and options are presented. Mechanisms and institutions that once were believed to be neutral with regard to outcomes are now being investigated to see what role they play in influencing individuals' decisions.

In this same vein, Bartels argues that the efficacy of framing effects in politics demonstrates that individuals do not have any stable political preferences; rather, they have what he calls "attitudes":

> In politics, as in other realms, responses to questions in opinion surveys and experiments—and referenda—are constructed from a disparate assortment of more or less relevant "considerations" [Zaller 1992], including bits and pieces of information, prototypes, slogans, and prejudices. The psychological mechanisms underlying attitude construction generate a variety of systematic and predictable violations of familiar axioms of preference consistency and stability, including preference reversals, question-ordering effects, anchoring effects, and inconsistencies in responses involving magnitudes or probabilities. (Bartels 2003a, 50)

Next, he claims that responsiveness to preferences is an essential part of liberal democratic theory. "Preferences lie close to the heart of liberal democratic theory. That fact is evident from the first page of Robert Dahl's classic study *Polyarchy*, which stipulated that 'a key characteristic of a democracy is the continued responsiveness of the government to the preferences of its citizens, considered as political equals' [Dahl 1971, 1]" (Bartels 2003a, 50).

Bartels concludes that framing effects undermine the view that citizens have political preferences to which democratic governments could or should be responsive. As a result, he proposes a number of alternatives for the future development of democratic theory: (1) Theorists could accept that democratic politics is nothing more than a "rhetorical free-for-all." On this view, media interests, political elites, and other powerful groups collectively determine the content of all political decisions, with voters playing an entirely passive role. (2) The empirical results could be taken to indicate that a normative account of frames must be developed. Bartels here insists that unless we can determine which frames are good and which are bad, then it will be impossible to rescue the idea that citizens have real (as opposed to merely expressed) preferences. Developing such a normative standard poses serious problems. (3) Democratic theory could reconcile itself to a weak form of democratic minimalism modeled on William Riker's claim that all citizens can do is exercise "an intermittent, sometimes random, even perverse, popular veto" (Riker

1982a, 244). Here, Bartels draws an analogy between Kenneth Arrow's celebrated "general possibility theorem"[37] and framing effects, claiming that both show the incoherence of the notion of "popular rule."

There are problems with each of these proposals, but I will focus here on two general concerns about Bartels's appropriation of the empirical literature on framing. First, he seriously overstates the strength of the empirical results concerning preference construction. Even in behavioral economics, where Kahneman and Tversky have been most influential, the construction of preferences has not been taken to entail that all choices are *uniquely* dependent on the context of elicitation. Instead, revealed preferences arise as the result of interplay between endogenous and exogenous forces. That is, choice is determined by factors both internal to, and external to the context of choice. The rejection of purely exogenous preferences is not equivalent to the conclusion that all choices are completely labile. Sunstein states this clearly: "Moreover, to say that a preference is endogenous is not to say that it is a mere whim or fancy, or highly malleable. Some preferences are in fact relatively stable, even if they are a function of legal rules, social pressures or existing institutions" (Sunstein 1992, 297–298n).

As a result, the image of all voters as passive, easily manipulated stooges is misleading. Instead, the empirical literature indicates that different frames appeal to an individual's divergent interests, considerations, and principles. Individuals who do not have stable preferences about a given issue may thus be inclined toward different choices depending on which considerations are emphasized. Susceptibility to framing does not indicate that choices are entirely determined by the process of elicitation but rather that choice is influenced by more factors than just preferences. As a result, Bartels's conclusions (especially his first alternative) overstate the importance of framing for democratic theory. Framing effects surely demonstrate that in some instances, human decisions fail to live up to the rational choice principle of invariance, but that does not entail that all preferences are manipulable. One of the most exciting areas of behavioral research (in economics, law, and decision theory) involves the generation of normative accounts of "preference management" (see Lichtenstein and Slovic 2006, part 9). This research attempts to determine how, given our susceptibility to framing effects, we can organize and improve our

---

[37] Also referred to as Arrow's "impossibility theorem." This theorem (Arrow 1951) showed that it is impossible to aggregate individual preferences into a social ordering that respects the constraints of unrestricted domain, the weak Pareto principle, nondictatorship, and the independence of irrelevant alternatives. This has proven to be a watershed result for social choice theory. Stated less abstractly, this theorem purports to show that any rule for generating a social choice from a collection of individual preferences will inevitably fail to respect at least one of a number of plausible logical requirements. For an analysis of this theorem, see *Choice, Welfare, and Measurement* (Sen 1999a).

choices. Such normative accounts are intelligible only if in fact we have some stable preferences and they are capable of being rendered consistent with the rest of our sometimes-variable choices.[38]

Second, even if we interpret the empirical results in the way that Bartels suggests, his proposals for reforming democratic theory are relevant only to preference-based theories of democracy. In particular, his account asserts that democracy is essentially a matter of reflecting individual preferences, where preferences are defined in the terms of classical economics. For this reason, Bartels is right to connect this criticism to Arrow's general possibility theorem. Both the kind of criticism he launched and Arrow's formal result are aimed primarily, if not exclusively, at theories of democracy that interpret votes as voter preferences.

There are a number of reasons, however, that we might be skeptical about theories of democracy that focus on preferences in this way. David Estlund has argued that preferences fail to meet the conditions of aggregability, advocacy, and activity that are required of any adequate interpretation of voting (Estlund 1990). Estlund has also soundly criticized preference-based theories that attempt to ground responsiveness to preferences in an ideal of procedural fairness (Estlund 2008, chap. 4). Further, preference-based theories of democracy still have to explain why government responsiveness to individual preferences is normatively desirable.

From another perspective, Geoffrey Brennan and Loren Lomasky have argued that the standard economic analysis of voting in terms of preferences fails to capture the predominantly expressive function of electoral behavior. They claim that it is a mistake to construe the relationship between preferences and choices in a democracy on the economic model. Because a voter's choice (unlike a consumer's) does not alone determine the outcome, voting is more akin to cheering for one's favorite sports team than it is like choosing to purchase a product (Brennan and Lomasky 1993). This insight greatly complicates the understanding of the relationship between preferences and choices that lies at the heart of preference-based theories of democracy.[39]

Finally, deliberative theories of democracy have criticized preference-based accounts for failing to recognize the importance of the conditions that lead to the formation of preferences in a democracy. Deliberative

---

[38] A related response to Bartels might make use of Dean Lacy's notion of nonseparable preferences (2001a and 2001b) to show that our preferences may not be as unstable as they initially appear. Lacy argues that much apparent preference instability is actually a result of causal linkages between alternatives. Survey responses may thus indicate that respondents are more responsive to issue framing than is actually the case. I thank an anonymous reviewer for bringing this possibility to my attention.

[39] For an account of these complications, see *Democratic Devices and Desires* (Brennan and Hamlin 2000).

theories emphasize the importance of designing just political procedures and practices that ensure that democratic decisions are legitimate (Gutmann and Thompson 1996; Habermas 1996). Thus, Bartels's decision to interpret framing effects in terms of their relevance to preferences greatly limits his account. Even if we accept his polemical characterization of framing effects, his three proposals only apply to theories of democracy that have been widely criticized for independent reasons. As a result, Bartels fails to provide a convincing account of the relevance of framing effects to normative democratic theory.

1.3.2 The Problem of Elite Manipulation

James Druckman has argued that emphasis framing effects are relevant to political philosophy primarily because citizens' susceptibility to framing leaves them vulnerable to manipulation by political elites.[40] Further, Druckman has investigated the possibility that various cultural and institutional mechanisms might reduce the effects of framing. His results have been mixed, but the picture he presents is substantially less pessimistic than the one offered by Bartels.

On this account, framing effects in general, and emphasis framing effects in particular, are taken to represent a possible failure of citizen competence. According to Druckman, if preferences are the product of elite manipulation, then citizens are incompetent. To see why this is the case, we must note that he (like Bartels) follows Robert Dahl (1971, 1) in asserting that the continuing responsiveness of government to the preferences of citizens is an essential characteristic of democracy (Druckman 2001b, 232). As a result, Druckman requires that the preferences of citizens be their own and not the result of manipulation. For him, framing effects are of concern because they represent a possible means of manipulating preferences:

> Most agree that emphasis framing effects also occur with some regularity—for example, Chong [1993, 870] explains that these types of framing effects constitute the "essence of political opinion formation." Indeed, much of politics involves battles over how a campaign, a problem, or an issue should be understood. This can be seen in debates over issues such as campaign finance (free speech or democratic corruption?), abortion (rights of mother or rights of unborn child?), gun control (right to bear arms or public safety?), affirmative action (reverse discrimination or remedial action?), welfare policy (humanitarianism

---

[40] In particular, see "Political Preference Formation: Competition, Deliberation, and the (Ir)relevance of Framing Effects" (Druckman 2004). For similar concerns, see Entman (1993, 2003); Simon and Xenos (2000).

or overspending?), hate group rallies (free speech or public safety?) and many more [Freedman 2000]. (Druckman 2001b, 235)

In order to determine whether or not the existence of framing effects in politics entails that citizens' preferences are the result of manipulation, Druckman focuses on the psychological processes through which elite manipulation works. In particular, he claims that manipulation (in order to be distinguished from mere persuasion) must occur automatically, without the possibility of critical reflection. He states, "If elite influence occurs automatically such that citizens subconsciously form preferences in accordance with elite discourse, then citizens will nearly always be vulnerable to manipulation" (Druckman 2001b, 233). Thus, on Druckman's assessment, the relevance of framing effects for political theory depends critically on whether or not we are essentially passive with respect to frames: if we uncritically parrot whichever political frame we are exposed to, then political elites can be expected to have free rein over our preferences, and we cannot be deemed competent.

Given this understanding of framing effects and their possible relevance to political theory, Druckman conducted a number of studies to determine whether or not citizens are in fact passive with respect to frames. That is, he set out to test the hypothesis that framing effects work through automatic, subconscious processes. He speculated that if framing effects were, on the contrary, the result of deliberate processes, then they would be moderated by several mechanisms characteristic of rational deliberation. These mechanisms include the effects of source credibility (Druckman 2001c), competition between frames (Druckman 2001a; Druckman and Chong 2007), and group deliberation (Druckman and Nelson 2003).

He has found that the effects of framing are sometimes limited by these mechanisms. When presented by credible sources (e.g., Colin Powell or the *New York Times*) frames tend to be more effective than when the same frames are presented by noncredible sources (e.g., Jerry Springer or the *National Enquirer*).[41] When alternative frames are presented together (90 percent employment and 10 percent unemployment), framing effects are often greatly reduced (Druckman 2001a). Also, certain kinds of groups, when induced to deliberate, are substantially less susceptible to framing (Druckman 2004).

The fact that framing effects can be moderated by mechanisms such as these has led Druckman to conclude that framing effects do not operate via automatic, subconscious processes. Instead, he claims that framing effects are more akin to rational deliberation, and that as a result, they do not imply that citizens' preferences are always vulnerable to elite manipulation: "I argue that it is premature to abandon the concepts of

---

[41] These examples are Druckman's (2001c), not mine.

preferences and attitudes, and to accept the concomitant implications. My results show that framing effects depend in critical ways on context—as a result, framing effects appear to be neither robust nor particularly pervasive. Elite competition and heterogeneous discussions limit and often eliminate framing effects" (Druckman 2004, 683).

Druckman's results, however, are not entirely optimistic. In particular, the third mechanism discussed above, that of group deliberation, met with mixed results. In groups where individuals were exposed to different, competing frames (i.e., in heterogeneous groups) and then induced to deliberate, the effects of framing were significantly minimized. This is good news for Druckman, as it seems to indicate that rational deliberation moderates susceptibility to elite manipulation. However, in groups where nonexperts were exposed to the same frames (i.e., in homogenous groups) and then induced to deliberate, framing effects persisted:

> The message for deliberative theorists is that homogeneous discussions act as a double-edged sword: They work to eliminate framing effects among experts; however, to the extent that the effects persist, they stimulate and reinforce an overconfidence in framed preferences (e.g., groupthink). Deliberation might lead to justification for preferences, but this is not a positive outcome if the preferences are baseless. (Druckman 2004, 682)

This result is troubling for Druckman, because it lends credence to the view that the effects of framing effects do not resemble rational processes, and this supports the view that citizen's preferences (at least where competition between frames is scarce) will be susceptible to elite manipulation.[42]

Druckman's analysis is interesting owing to, among other things, its sober assessment of the empirical literature concerning framing effects. When contrasted with Bartels, Druckman presents a far more plausible account of both the pervasiveness of framing effects and the mechanisms that underlie the construction of preferences. It is important to note, however, that Druckman's definition of citizen competence in terms of nonmanipulation raises some important theoretical questions. In particular, he manages to avoid explaining why elite manipulation is bad by relying on a background democratic theory that construes responsiveness to citizen preferences as essential. It is only in this way that Druckman's focus on the kind of psychological process underlying susceptibility to framing makes sense. For, if we were to construe the import of democratic government instrumentally (i.e., the justification of democracy has to do with whether

---

[42] This result coincides with research conducted on the effects of group deliberation by Cass Sunstein and others (Sunstein 2000b, 2006; Schkade et al. 2007). Sunstein has found that when conditions of information homogeneity prevail, collective decisions tend to polarize, while, at the same time, confidence in those decisions reliably increases.

it produces certain results, rather than whether governments respond to preferences), then elite manipulation ceases to be obviously pernicious. It is at least possible that responsiveness to elite frames could, under certain conditions, conduce to better instrumental results. In this case, the psychological processes underlying framing effects would be irrelevant.

Now, I am not claiming that in fact elite manipulation of citizen's preferences is a good thing,[43] but we should acknowledge that Druckman fails to provide an adequate characterization of how theories of democracy that are not grounded in preferences should regard framing effects. Certainly, the fact that framing effects can be limited by certain institutional (or even cultural, in the case of group deliberation) mechanisms is relevant to other theories, but the manner in which these results connect to claims about citizen competence is unclear. For, unless we are wedded to the view that governments must defer to individual preferences (and, as we saw in the last section, there are reasons to divorce ourselves from such a view), then we still lack an account of why framing effects are normatively undesirable. Bartels lacks such an account, and so does Druckman.

1.3.3 The Anti-antipaternalism Argument

Recently, a different way of interpreting the empirical literature on framing effects has garnered a great deal of attention. Cass Sunstein and Richard Thaler have claimed that empirical results concerning the construction of preferences serve to counter many libertarian arguments against paternalism in public policy. On the basis of research from behavioral economics, they argue for what they call "libertarian paternalism."[44] The idea here is that our lack of stable preferences, in certain instances, opens up the possibility of adopting strategies that seek to make us better off (this is the paternalistic element of their proposal), without foreclosing any of our options (this is the libertarian element). This view has come under fire from a number of perspectives,[45] and it has also spurred some interesting applications of their thesis.[46]

---

[43] In the next section, however, I examine Cass Sunstein and Richard Thaler's suggestion that in certain situations, preference manipulation might be desirable.

[44] Sunstein and Thaler have received a great deal of attention for *Nudge: Improving Decisions about Health, Wealth, and Happiness* (2008), but more technical versions of the same argument were presented by the authors in "Libertarian Paternalism" (2003a) and "Libertarian Paternalism Is Not an Oxymoron" (2003b).

[45] Gregory Mitchell claims that the authors have misinterpreted the empirical literature (Mitchell 2005). Edward Glaeser claims that bureaucrats and other policy engineers are less likely to promote welfare than the individuals affected (Glaeser 2006). Daniel Klein criticizes libertarian paternalism for misconstruing the nature of paternalism (Klein 2004a, 2004b; Sunstein 2004b).

[46] Recent research has dealt with personal investments (Bernartzi and Thaler 2002), retirement savings (Camerer, Issacharoff, et al. 2003; Bernartzi and Thaler 2004), social

As Sunstein, Thaler, and Jolls claim in an earlier work, "bounded rationality pushes toward a sort of anti-antipaternalism—a skepticism about antipaternalism, but not an affirmative defense of paternalism" (Jolls, Sunstein, et al. 1998, 1541). Thus the form of paternalism embodied in libertarian paternalism is rather soft. They claim, on the basis of evidence of bounded rationality and self-control, that in some cases it is possible to reconcile freedom of choice with a weak form of paternalism. Here is one of their central examples:

> Consider the problem facing the director of a company cafeteria who discovers that the order in which food is arranged influences the choices people make. To simplify, consider three alternative strategies: (1) she could make choices that she thinks would make the customers best off; (2) she could make the choices at random; or (3) she could maliciously choose those items that she thinks would make the customers as obese as possible. Option 1 appears to be paternalistic, which it is, but would anyone advocate options 2 or 3? (Sunstein and Thaler 2003a, 175)

Sunstein and Thaler claim that the cafeteria director described above cannot help but make a choice that affects the decisions of her customers. Food must be arranged in some way, and the organizational strategy that is adopted will help to determine what people eat. The reason that this is the case stems from the (in this case, unproven) assertion that food ordering influences food choice. That is, we are invited to imagine that in this situation individuals lack clear, stable, or well-defined preferences about what to eat. Given this deficiency, an opportunity presents itself: the cafeteria director has the chance to promote better nutrition without having to eliminate any of her customer's options. Should she choose strategy 1, then more people will be induced to choose healthy options, but those with a well-defined preference for a cheeseburger and fries will not have had their freedom of choice restricted in any way.

The kind of paternalism advocated by Sunstein and Thaler is thus opportunistic: when individual preferences are not stable and it is possible to do so without impinging on freedom of choice, concern for individual welfare warrants the manipulation of individuals' choices. This is made possible by framing effects. Sunstein and Thaler expand on this account by invoking the related phenomenon of the status quo bias.[47] When an option is framed in terms of a deviation from the status quo, it tends to be greatly dispreferred when compared with frames that cast that same choice as the continuation of the current state of affairs

---

security (Cronqvist and Thaler 2004), cocaine addiction (Stevenson 2005), and the Medicare Part D prescription drug program (McFadden 2006).

[47] For our purposes here, I choose to interpret the status quo bias as a species of emphasis framing effect. I do so because it involves emphasizing different elements of a decision problem and affects eventual choices.

(Kahneman, Knetsch, et al. 2000a). Thus, people display a bias in favor of the status quo, even when there is no cost to changes from the current state. This is important because it is often the case that planners of various kinds have discretion with regard to which state of affairs comes to be regarded as the status quo. Sunstein and Thaler present the following example of the status quo bias:

> One illustration of this phenomenon comes from studies of automatic enrollment in 401(k) employee savings plans. Most 401(k) plans use an opt-in design. When employees first become eligible to participate in the 401(k) plan, they receive some plan information and an enrollment form that must be completed in order to join. Under the alternative of automatic enrollment, employees receive the same information, but are told that unless they opt out, they will be enrolled in the plan (with some default options for savings rates and asset allocation). In companies that offer a "match" (the employer matches the employee's contribution according to some formula, often a 50-percent match up to some cap), most employees eventually do join the plan, but the enrollments occur much sooner under automatic enrollment. For example, Brigitte Madrian and Dennis Shea [2001] found that initial enrollments jumped from 49 percent to 86 percent, and Choi, et al. [2002] find similar results for other companies. (Sunstein and Thaler 2003a, 176–177)

In this case, companies have the ability to decide which option will be defined as the status quo: enrollment or nonenrollment. Because individuals' preferences are not stable here, framing effects are inevitable: there is no way to structure options that is neutral with respect to the kinds of choices that will be made. Under either system, employees have the same alternatives, and so, according to Sunstein and Thaler, there is no plausible libertarian objection to either scheme. But given that whatever decision is made about the status quo will have substantial influence on how much individuals will save over the course of their careers, Sunstein and Thaler argue that companies ought to choose the opt-out design, privileging enrollment as the status quo. This, they claim, serves to promote the welfare of the employees (as they tend to save more). This choice on the part of companies is paternalistic: it is made with an eye toward steering employees toward decisions that promote their own welfare. Sunstein and Thaler conclude that, in situations like this one, the choice of frame ought to be made on the basis of welfarist considerations.

We should note that this argument provides a plausible candidate for Bartels's second proposal (see section 1.3.1). That is, Sunstein and Thaler here provide a normative account of frames in terms of welfare: frames ought to be judged good or bad, better or worse, depending on what influence they will have on the welfare of those affected. Because Sunstein and Thaler intend the account sketched here to apply to all "sensible planners"—human resource directors, bureaucrats, and kings inclusive (Sunstein and Thaler 2003a, 178)—I take it to be appropriate that we apply their analysis to the case of normative democratic theory. In particular, it seems fitting to ask whether this line of reasoning licenses politicians, pundits, or oligarchs (i.e., Druckman's political elites) to engage in the manipulation of citizen preferences.

According to Sunstein and Thaler, when framing effects are inevitable and no options are precluded by the choice of frame, then those who have the opportunity should select the frame that best serves to promote the welfare of those affected. One of the problems with Sunstein and Thaler's view, however, is that their endorsement of paternalism with regard to frames seems to open the door to various forms of error, abuse, and profiteering.

Sunstein and Thaler make it clear that in situations where freedom of choice is respected and framing is unavoidable, individuals ought to frame choices in ways that they *think* will promote the welfare of those affected. It is important to note, however, that in these instances we already have concerns about the ability of those affected to reliably choose what is in their own interest (as their preferences are unstable). As a result, Sunstein and Thaler seem to trust designers and planners more than they trust run-of-the-mill choosers. Libertarian forms of paternalism will sometimes involve error, where planners choose frames in a way that they think will promote the interests of those affected, but in fact does not. This kind of error seems to be unavoidable. If the argument for libertarian paternalism is carried over to the framing of political issues in a democracy, then we must acknowledge that issues would sometimes be improperly framed.

There is, on this account, also the possibility that designers will engage in paternalism when in fact no paternalism is necessary. As we saw above, Sunstein and Thaler claim that two conditions need to be met in order to satisfy the libertarian paternalist: no options should be precluded and framing effects must be inevitable (because preferences are unstable). However, there are ways (recall Druckman's credibility, counterframing, and group deliberation experiments) to eliminate framing effects. By altering the situation in which choices occur, it is sometimes possible to stabilize people's preferences. If designers too readily engage in libertarian forms of paternalism, then they may miss opportunities to eliminate framing effects. In the democratic context, this kind of abuse would result in voters being treated paternalistically when no paternalism was required.

We should note also that, if libertarian paternalism is accepted, cases of profiteering would surely occur. As an example, take the above-described cafeteria director and her decision regarding which strategy to use in organizing her customers' choices. There are surely more strategies available to her than just the three outlined by the authors.[48] Most obviously, the cafeteria director could also arrange her inventory so as to maximize profits.[49] That is, she could feature items that are old, overpriced, or overstocked early in the line. Although this would satisfy the libertarian requirement, it would not constitute paternalism, as she would not be promoting the health or well-being of her customers. Instead, she would seem to be engaging in a kind of profiteering, securing her personal benefit by capitalizing on the instability of other people's preferences.[50] This seems particularly likely to occur in democratic politics, where both power and wealth can tempt planners away from acting paternalistically.

From the perspective of political philosophy, however, there is something more troubling than just the error, abuse, and profiteering that is likely to follow from Sunstein and Thaler's version of paternalism. This problem results from the fact that Sunstein and Thaler do not actually argue for welfare being the only relevant criterion for evaluating frames—they simply assume that it is. There are, however, a number of different criteria that could be used to evaluate frames. For one, designers could choose frames, not on the basis of what would promote the welfare of those directly affected (e.g., the interests of cafeteria customers), but rather on the basis of what would promote overall utility (i.e., the interests of the wider world of customers and noncustomers). It is clear that if designers pursue this strategy, they would not be acting paternalistically, but they might still be acting in a morally laudatory way. This would be a form of libertarian utilitarianism, rather than libertarian paternalism.

And it doesn't end there. We can also construct versions of the libertarian argument that claim that our choice of frame should be made, not on the basis of welfare or overall utility, but rather on the basis of considerations of justice. That is, we could argue for a thesis that claims: In instances where individuals do not have stable preferences and where the choice of frame does not curtail anyone's options, those with the opportunity ought to select the frame that, in their estimation, serves to promote policies that

---

[48] In "Libertarian Paternalism Is Not an Oxymoron," Sunstein and Thaler list a fourth strategy: "She could give consumers what she thinks they would choose on their own" (2003b, 1165).

[49] In *Nudge* (2008, 2), they admit the possibility of maximizing profits or even bribes. As we will see below, there are many other possible options.

[50] This kind of profiteering seems to me the most predictable result of the heuristics and biases research. Already, the influence on marketing and financial strategies is unmistakable. See, for example *Why Smart People Make Big Money Mistakes and How to Correct Them: Lessons from the Life-Changing Science of Behavioral Economics* (Belsky and Gilovich 2010).

comply with Rawls's two principles of justice.[51] As an example, take the situation of a legislator drafting a referendum proposing to raise property taxes. Imagine that the legislator knows that people are affected by the status quo bias, and she must decide between two formulations of the proposal: (i) proposing "a 2 percent increase over last year's taxes" (a deviation from the status quo) or (ii) proposing to "maintain the same rate of increase as in previous years" (a continuation of the status quo). Because continuing the status quo is likely to be preferred to the deviation frame, her choice could influence the referendum results. Let's assume that our legislator believes it to be the case that it is in the interest of voters to have lower property taxes. If she follows Sunstein and Thaler's advice, then she will select formulation (i), as it may incline voters with unstable preferences to vote against the increase. But let us also assume that she believes it to be the case that higher property taxes serve to improve the condition of the worst-off citizens. If she chooses to evaluate the two formulations on the basis of what effect they will have on justice (as described by Rawls), then she will select formulation (ii), as it nudges those with unstable preferences toward endorsing the proposed increase.

This example is intended to show that the manipulation of frames in a democracy (even when motivated by moral principles and constrained by a libertarian respect for the freedom to choose) is a complicated affair.[52] Just as there is controversy about what kinds of distributive strategies ought to be pursued in politics (e.g., welfare maximization or maximin principles of justice), there will be controversy about how we ought to evaluate competing formulations of political questions and issues. Thus, even if we ignore the likelihood of error, abuse, and profiteering, Sunstein and Thaler's paternalism reveals a whole host of problems concerning how framing effects ought to be handled in a democracy. Unfortunately, their straightforwardly welfarist proposal is not convincing, and it is unclear whether any proposal for the evaluation of frames will be generally acceptable. What does seem clear, however, is that there is ample opportunity for manipulation of citizens' preferences in a democracy and that, moreover, this manipulation might not always be morally objectionable.

1.4 FRAMING EFFECTS AND POLITICAL JUDGMENT

I think normative democratic theory ought to develop a different construal of framing effects. This construal, which I see as an important part of a behavioral approach to democratic theory, will be described more

---

[51] See John Rawls's *A Theory of Justice* (1999b).

[52] I develop these issues further in "Libertarian Paternalism, Utilitarianism, and Justice" (Kelly, forthcoming).

fully in subsequent chapters (especially chapters 3 and 4). For now, it is important to note two things. First, I take it to be the case that existing empirical studies have established that much human decision making violates the rational choice principle of invariance. Second, I advocate replacing this principle (which claims that choices will be invariant across different presentations of the same decision-making problem) with an understanding of decision variance imported from the heuristics and biases literature. Thus, I think we should expect many individuals to respond differently to frames that emphasize different elements of a given choice scenario.[53] In this way, we can use existing psychological research as a replacement for the rational choice principle of invariance. As a result, I will claim that for the purposes of normative democratic theory, we ought to assume that frames for political decisions will (in some unspecified number of instances) affect the choices that individuals make and that we should look to empirical research to determine how particular frames will influence these choices.

This construal of the phenomenon of framing effects and its relevance for political philosophy, I contend, ought to lead us to reevaluate the role and importance of individual political judgment in democratic decision making. In what follows, I will focus on the impact of framing effects on the judgment of citizens, rather than on their preferences. My concern is that the tendency of our decisions to be swayed by frames might undermine the reliability of our political judgment. I argue that we should be concerned that framing effects will lead democracies to make political judgments that are substantively incorrect. As a result of these considerations, normative theories of democracy ought to account for how our susceptibility to framing affects the reliability of democratic judgments.

1.5 Four Objections

In order to develop my account further, I will here present and respond to a number of general objections to my construal of the relevance of framing effects for democratic theory. In particular, I consider four objections to interpreting framing effects as a threat to the reliability of political judgment. I hope that my responses to these challenges will help to flesh out my construal of the relationship between framing effects and democratic theory.

---

[53] For example, the empirical literature on framing effects indicates that we are more responsive to frames that emphasize losses rather than gains. This claim, and many related ones, are derived from Kahneman and Tversky's research on framing (Kahneman and Tversky 2000a, 2000d).

1.5.1 All Frames Are Equal

One important objection to my argument interprets the empirical evidence of framing in a very radical way. It begins by claiming that the evidence of framing effects ought to lead us to abandon the idea that there is anything other than frames to which our judgments are responsive: on this account, our judgments are responsive to frames and nothing but frames.[54]

This objection then goes on to make a further claim, rejecting my assertion that we should worry about the possibility that framing effects might negatively affect our judgments. If there is nothing but frames to which judgment is responsive, as this view holds, then it appears to follow that all frames are equal.[55] Because framing effects alone seem to determine the content of our judgments, this objection claims that there can be no reason to prefer one frame to another. This view thus concludes that if all frames are equal, there is no threat to political judgment; there is nothing to worry about here.

An important consequence of this objection is the rejection of the idea that we should be responsive to reasons, as opposed to frames. If all frames are equal, and there is nothing that objectively recommends one frame rather than another, then it seems as if there is no role to be played by reasons in influencing our judgment. There would be no reason why we should be responsive to a particular frame, and no grounds on which we could criticize others for being swayed by a given way of framing an issue.

In order to be convincing, however, I take it that this objection relies on a kind of normative skepticism about judgment. More specifically, it requires that we concede that there are no objective norms governing our judgments. It is only if we deny that some judgments are objectively better than others that we are led to the conclusion that all frames are equal. More than just empirically asserting that human judgment is only responsive to framing, this objection thus requires that we deny that there are any standards to which human judgment *ought* to be responsive.

---

[54] It should be possible to argue on empirical grounds against this assertion (e.g., by showing that we are responsive to considerations other than frames), but this will not be my strategy here. I take it that there is nothing in this very radical interpretation of the empirical evidence that is hostile to my approach. As a result, I need not take a stance on this issue. It is only if one takes the step outlined in the next paragraph that one develops an objection to my view.

[55] It should be noted that nothing of the sort actually does follow. We cannot jump from the purported fact that we are only responsive to frames to the normative conclusion that we *ought* only be responsive to frames. Thus, I will argue, we should not accept the claim that all frames are equal.

Whatever we make of the empirical assertion,[56] I think we should reject this normative claim.

In what follows I assume that there are, at least some of the time, independent standards against which we must evaluate the correctness of our judgments. The content of these standards may vary with the context, but I take it that our judgments ought to be evaluated in terms of standards such as truth, morality, or justice.[57] Some judgments are correct whereas others are incorrect, and some judgments are better or worse than others—with regard to these standards. Furthermore, the standards that determine the correctness of our judgments are independent of our beliefs and preferences. As a result, I am committed to the view that all frames are not equal: some dispose us to make good decisions; others dispose us to make bad ones.

Reasons, on my account, are just whatever it is that we would be responsive to (in the circumstances) if we made substantively correct judgments. That is, a reason is just whatever we ought to be responsive to, given the standards governing our judgments. Framing effects are pernicious when they lead us to make judgments on the basis of considerations other than reasons, because they thereby cause us to make judgments that do not accord with the evaluative standards that apply to them.

This is an admittedly abstract way of thinking about judgment (and about reasons), but the upshot of this way of approaching the issue is that it allows us to avoid normative skepticism without being forced to endorse the unrealistic assumptions of the rational actor model. We can acknowledge that there are normative standards governing our judgments, and that framing effects can affect our responsiveness to these standards,[58] but we avoid making any unrealistic assertions about our actual cognitive performance.

[56] Given the analysis of reasons below, this empirical claim might be interpreted to mean that whenever we are responsive to a reason, we are also responding to a frame, or it might be interpreted to mean that we are never responsive to reasons. The former interpretation seems to me quite plausible, whereas the latter seems to be empirically unverifiable. Unfortunately, these issues would lead us too far afield, so I will not pursue them further.

[57] For many contemporary theories of democracy, standards of truth dominate. In particular, epistemic theories of democracy are focused on the ability of democracies to make judgments that correspond to the truth about politics. As a result, in chapters 2 and 4, I will focus a great deal on how framing effects impact our ability to seek the truth in politics. However, I have structured my response above in such a way that it is not committed to any specific understanding of the proper standards governing our judgments.

[58] Further, we can see that framing effects are not necessarily pernicious: frames are only bad when they lead us to make judgments that are incorrect. When the framing of a decision leads us to be sensitive to the reasons that ought to apply in that circumstance, then there is no epistemic downside to our sensitivity to framing.

In order to reject my response to this objection, the normative skeptic must claim that no objective standards govern our judgments. This, I think, is an extremely radical conclusion, one that is certainly not warranted by empirical evidence of framing effects. My account requires us to acknowledge the role of truth or morality or justice in governing some (but not all) of our decisions, but it does not require that we agree about the content of these standards or what they demand in any given case.

Before I leave this objection behind, it might be helpful to consider a more concrete (and controversial) version of my response:[59] one very common reply to the skeptic is that human judgment ought to be responsive to the truth.[60] That is, we ought to make true judgments. On this account, we should understand the normative standards governing judgment in terms of truth and falsity: judgments are correct when they are true, and they are incorrect when they are false. Further, human judgment is reliable when it can be generally trusted to make true judgments, and it is unreliable if it generally makes false judgments. Reasons, on this account, can simply be defined as truth-indicators (e.g., we might say that reasons provide good evidence for holding a certain belief). In other words, what is distinctive about reasons is that we ought to be responsive to them because they provide us with a guide to the truth. This, I assume, is an appealing, if somewhat controversial way of thinking about the standards that govern judgment.[61] Framing effects would thus be pernicious when they lead us to make judgments on the basis of considerations other than the truth.[62]

The account of framing effects that I defend in this book therefore rejects normative skepticism. I take it that there are objective standards that govern our judgments (in many instances truth may provide the relevant standard, but in others morality or justice may apply) and that

[59] I do not wish to commit myself to the specific claims presented in this paragraph, but I hope it will help to clarify the structure of my answer to the normative skeptic.

[60] For example, both David Estlund (2008) and Robert Talisse (2009a) construct their theories of democracy around this sort of assertion.

[61] In particular, this way of thinking about judgment is controversial because it might be committed to a specific thesis in epistemology: conceiving of reasons as truth-indicators may entail a commitment to a kind of epistemological externalism. It should be remembered, however, that this is just one way of understanding the proper normative standards that govern individual judgment. Alternatively, it should be possible understand truth in terms of consistency (yielding an epistemological position more friendly to epistemological internalists) or a range of other standards (including rightness, justice, or what have you). The larger argument of this book is agnostic on this issue, as there are a number of ways we might go about filling in the details of my response.

[62] It is important to note, however, that our responsiveness to frames does not necessarily reduce the accuracy of our judgments. If our responsiveness to frames were successfully mobilized in the service of truth, then it would be entirely possible that framing effects would help, rather than hinder us in making accurate judgments.

we ought to be responsive to these standards. For the sake of my argument, all that one needs to concede is that some judgments are correct and others incorrect, that some judgments are better than others. In an effort to be ecumenical, I will not specify in any detail the proper way of understanding the standards governing judgment, but I am committed to the view that all frames are not equal. In what follows, I will say that individual judgments are accurate when they are correct (i.e., when they respond to the norms properly placed on judgment) and that human judgment is reliable if it is generally capable of making correct judgments. Further, I will take reasons to be whatever we should be responsive to in order to make correct judgments. In any given case it might be impossible for us to distinguish between frames and reasons (this, indeed, is the central difficulty raised by framing effects), but this should not itself lead us to skepticism. Instead, we ought to recognize the extent of the difficulty presented by our responsiveness to frames and strive to determine ways in which we can become more responsive to reasons.

1.5.2 Frames in the Wild

A second objection might argue that, in the absence of deliberate manipulation, framing effects will be inconsequential for democratic politics. In its wild state, it could be argued, politics would be uncorrupted by frames: different frames for political issues, randomly distributed within political debate and decision making, would cancel each other out once individual judgments are aggregated. On this view, we should only be concerned with framing effects insofar as there is evidence of a widespread and successful initiative to skew frames in a direction that would lead us to make judgments that were substantively incorrect. In the absence of such systematic biases, it could be argued that we ought to assume that politics remains in its wild state, and that we should therefore be unconcerned about the influence of framing effects on the judgment of individuals or groups.

This kind of response, however, requires both an unduly naive view of the nature of democratic politics and an overly conspiratorial understanding of how frames might come to be manipulated. Within any representative system of democracy (and perhaps also any system of direct democracy that incorporates public debate), the widespread framing of political issues seems inevitable. So long as political issues remain complex and political messages are disseminated on a mass scale, the regular framing of decisions is an important (and perhaps indispensable) simplifying device for public debate and discussion. Framing issues in memorable ways is not always a cynical attempt at sophistry: even honest attempts to explain and present political issues will require that individuals make use of frames. So long as the presentation of political issues and attempts at political persuasion are carried out in an organized manner, politics will involve the systematization of political messages.

The widespread framing of issues, then, does not require the deliberate activity of some group bent on the subversion of democratic judgment (we should note, however, that it does not preclude such deliberate subversion either). Even in its most pristine form, political debate in large societies will include the dissemination of issues framed in particular ways.[63] Further, even when the framing of political issues is carried out with the very best of intentions (as we saw in the case of libertarian paternalism), there will be controversy about whether the choice of a given frame is inappropriately skewing political debate. In light of the seemingly obligatory nature of frames and the fact that their use is not always condemnable, I cannot see how frames for political issues could ever be randomly distributed. In the absence of such a random distribution, however, we must expect framing to have some kind of effect (whether positive or negative) on democratic decision making. The extent of this influence and its importance will depend on the degree of our susceptibility to frames, but framing effects must have some kind of influence on political judgments in a democracy.[64]

1.5.3 Apples and Oranges

A third way of objecting to the importance of framing effects for judgment-based theories of democracy is to claim that the existing empirical literature does not suffice to show that frames cause individuals to make mistaken political judgments. Those proposing such an objection need not claim that framing effects are incapable of causing such mistakes; they might simply claim that there is not yet sufficient empirical evidence to warrant concerns about framing in political judgment. On this view, worries about framing effects are premature: until more relevant evidence is produced, we ought not waste our time worrying about these issues.

---

[63] Perhaps, if in very small societies political debate were to be carried out in a deliberately unorganized way, politics might be wild enough to make framing inconsequential. In such a condition, individuals would have to decide not to characterize issues in standardized ways. This anarchist possibility, however, is so very distant from the character of contemporary politics that I will put it aside for the purposes for my discussion.

[64] Further, anyone with a sufficiently liberal political outlook ought to desire a large number of frames for political issues. Because only the deliberate use of force seems capable of constricting frames, we should expect any palatably liberal society to have a high degree of diversity. In such a condition, however, our susceptibility to framing will inevitably have some influence on political judgment.

This objection is plausible because relatively few studies have been dedicated to documenting the influence of framing effects on political judgment. Numerous studies have documented the relationship between framing effects and the instability of political preferences and decisions, but very few have attempted to show that the manner in which a political issue is framed can cause individuals to make judgments that are straightforwardly incorrect. There are a number of reasons for the dearth of empirical evidence directly addressing the reliability of political judgment.

First, the disciplines that have been responsible for the bulk of the research on framing effects are focused on issues other than politics.[65] Economists studying framing effects have been most interested in the influence of framing on individuals' assessment of financial risk (Kahneman and Lovallo 2000; Shafir, Diamond, et al. 2000; Thaler 2000c) and utility (Kahneman 2000; Lowenstein and Adler 2000; Tversky and Griffin 2000). Legal theorists have been concerned with the relationship between issue framing and legal decisions (Cohen and Knetsch 2000; McCaffery et al. 2002), as well as the design of laws (Sunstein and Thaler 2003b; Nash 2006). Some social scientists have attempted to study the role of framing effects in politics (Bartels 2003a; Druckman 2004), but have done so with a focus on preference instability rather than judgment error. As a result, there exists little data that directly documents the impact of framing effects on the accuracy of our political judgments.

The area in which framing effects have been most commonly shown to negatively affect individual judgment concerns probabilistic reasoning. Researchers working in the heuristics and biases tradition have identified a number of anomalies (Kahneman, Knetsch, et al. 2000a), fallacies (Tversky and Kahneman 1983), and errors (Goodie and Fantino 1996), that characterize human judgments about probability. Many of these mistakes involve framing (Johnson, Hershey, et al. 2000; Thaler 2000b; Tversky 2000).[66] In these areas, individual judgments about probability are evaluated against a normative standard supplied by either expected utility theory (Von Neumann and Morgenstern 1944) or Bayesian probability theory (Bayes 1764) and are found to be lacking. These probabilistic mistakes have been taken by many to be the most robust evidence of the pernicious effect of cognitive biases on human reasoning (Bishop and Trout 2005).

---

[65] Similarly, there here has been relatively little analysis of framing effects in ethics (Petrinovich and O'Neill 1996; Sunstein 2004a; Sinnott-Armstrong 2008), or in epistemology (Gold and List 2004; Bishop and Trout 2005).

[66] Judgment errors caused by hindsight (Gulati et al. 2004) and optimism (Armour and Taylor 2002) biases have been particularly important for behavioral approaches to law (Jolls 2006). These biases, however, appear to be unrelated to framing effects.

It should be noted, however, that even in these areas, there has been controversy as to whether the apparent deviations from expected utility or Bayesianism ought to be construed as errors.[67] Some have claimed that human probabilistic reasoning ought to be evaluated in light of its ecological context or evolutionary history (Gigerenzer 2008). Others have claimed that a proper understanding of the normative standards in question reveals that there is in fact no real conflict with human probabilistic reasoning (Levi 1985; Hintikka 2004). As a result of these and other objections, a number of questions remain about how to identify and quantify judgment errors caused by framing (McKenzie 2004; Sher and McKenzie 2006).

For my purposes here, I will take it to have been established that, at least to some (again unspecified) extent, framing effects can negatively affect our political judgments. I assume that the accuracy of human judgment is dependent on our being responsive to good reasons. That is, our ability to make correct judgments is dependent on our being responsive to reasons in favor of that judgment. Insofar as the empirical literature has established that human judgment is responsive to framing, then to that extent, our judgment is responsive to something other than reasons. From this, I think we can infer that our judgments, when influenced by frames, are not entirely reliable. The empirical literature on framing does not yet indicate how unreliable our judgment might be, but I contend that the emerging evidence on framing effects gives us ample reason to believe that the framing of political issues sometimes negatively affects our political judgment.

The strength of my response to this objection rests on straightforwardly empirical issues. If further investigation reveals that framing effects do not significantly impair the accuracy of political judgment, then the response sketched here will be ineffective. That is, if researchers determine that our political judgments are only rarely affected by framing or that the effects of framing are not damaging to group judgments, then framing effects should have no appreciable impact on normative democratic theory. As a result, the argument developed in the remainder of this book hinges on one important empirical premise: human beings are susceptible to the effects of framing in a way that significantly and negatively affects the accuracy of our judgment about political issues. If this premise turns out to be false (and it could), then the behavioral approach (at least insofar as it is concerned with framing effects) will have nothing interesting to contribute to normative democratic theory. Given the current abundance of empirical evidence of framing effects, however, this seems an unlikely prospect.

[67] See especially the controversy over base rates (J. Koehler 1993; Fletcher 1994).

1.5.4 Politics Is Not Sui Generis

One last way of objecting to my construal of the relationship between framing effects and political judgment is to claim that I am committed to the implausible view that there is something special about politics that makes us particularly vulnerable to the effects of framing. If, in fact, there is nothing special about political judgment (i.e., political issues are continuous with moral, professional, and personal decisions), then we should be no more worried about framing effects in politics than we are about their influence on human judgment in general.

In response to this objection, I concede that there is nothing special about politics that makes us particularly vulnerable to framing effects. As I am using the term here, "politics" simply picks out a set of issues and questions that are of particular public concern. The content of this set is quite variable, and I do not want to specify it in any detail. Further, I think we *should* be concerned that framing effects might undermine human judgment concerning all sorts of issues. Whether we are making judgments about politics, science, or our personal lives, I think the empirical evidence strongly supports the view that our judgments are likely to be responsive to frames. To the extent that our judgments are swayed by something other than good reasons, I think we should worry about their accuracy. This is true in gambling, dating, cooking, and any other human endeavor where we might be concerned about having good judgment. Even if we view our susceptibility to framing as constant across all domains of human judgment, however, there are at least two reasons for being particularly concerned about their effect on political decision making.

First, it should be noted that in other areas where we are collectively interested in making good judgments, there are usually a whole set of norms and institutions in place that serve to reduce the incidence and impact of framing. For example, within scientific and other academic contexts where we are collectively interested in seeking the truth, we rely on large-scale institutional arrangements for vetting our judgments and improving our decisions. We make use of peer and blind review to ensure the quality of published work, and we depend on hiring and tenure committees to select those who are capable of making important contributions to our collective projects. Mechanisms such as these also provide motivation for improving our judgment. In other domains, market incentives, schemes of quality control, managerial oversight, and other systems for improving our judgment are employed in order to ensure that we, collectively, are better able to make good judgments. Many of these mechanisms seem to be effective means of ensuring that frames do not improperly sway our judgments. For a whole host of reasons, however, most such norms and institutions are conspicuously absent from democratic politics. As a result, we seem to be particularly ill-equipped to deal with the effects of framing in politics.

Second, we ought to be more concerned with making correct judgments in politics than regarding most other issues. Insofar as politics deals with matters that are of collective concern, we should be particularly attentive to the reliability of our judgments about these issues. Furthermore, the seriousness and enormous consequence of many political questions warrants a heightened concern about the correctness of our decisions. The fact that questions about rights, the distribution of public goods, and the use of coercive force are all (at least indirectly) subject to our collective political judgment in a democracy justifies an increased concern about the prevalence of framing effects.

In this way, I agree that we should reject the view that politics is entirely distinct from other areas of human inquiry. Instead, I think that we should be (and in many cases are already) concerned with the accuracy of our judgments across a whole range of domains. In politics, however, the stakes are higher, and there is a paucity of mechanisms capable of helping us improve our judgment. Thus, I do not contend that there is something peculiar about politics that makes our judgment more vulnerable to frames. Instead, I am arguing only that we dedicate the degree of concern to our political judgment that the high stakes of democratic politics deserves.

CHAPTER TWO

Theories of Democracy

BEFORE WE CAN FURTHER DEVELOP the behavioral approach, however, we need to pause awhile in order to contend with the current state of normative democratic theory. As things stand, there exists no single, unified field of research on democracy or democratic government. Instead, there are a number of individual disciplines and subdisciplines, each treating democracy in its own particular way.[1] Further adding to our difficulties, these disciplines have by now produced an astounding number of distinct, interconnected, and sometimes redundant theories of democracy. As a result, despite the benefits of terminological simplicity, if we are being careful, we should not speak of "democratic theory" but rather of "theories of democracy."

The line of reasoning developed in this book should therefore be understood as a behavioral approach to theories of democracy. Given the current diversity of these theories, however, it is difficult to know how to address such a huge collection of ideas. In order to make things more manageable, I will here develop a taxonomy of theories of democracy that maps the extent to which they rely on the judgment of citizens. I hope to achieve two things by doing this. First, I want to sort the vast array of extant theories of democracy into a smaller number of useful, descriptive categories. Second, I hope that these categories will be instructive for my specific purposes insofar as they reflect the extent to which the phenomenon of framing effects will be regarded as damaging to particular theories of democracy.

In what follows, I will take it to be the case that theories of democracy that depend less on the judgments of citizens ought to be less concerned about framing effects than those theories that depend more on citizens' having reliable political judgment. In order to clarify the differences between these theories, I propose a spectrum of epistemic demands: at the low end there are minimalist theories of democracy—those that make few, if any, demands on the correctness of individual judgments.[2] At the

---

[1] For example, research in democratic theory is regularly undertaken in philosophy, political science, political theory, legal theory, economics, social psychology, anthropology, history, and any number of smaller disciplines.

[2] A warning is in order here: the sense in which I am using the term "minimalist" is related to, but different from, the way it is used by thinkers such as Adam Przeworski

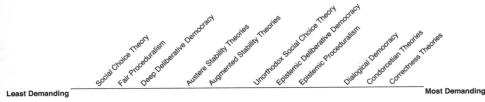

Figure 1. Epistemic demands of theories of democracy.

other end of the spectrum there are epistemic theories of democracy—those that demand that citizens in a democracy be capable of making substantively correct political judgments.[3]

For the purposes of my taxonomy, I will ignore whether the views presented here are at all convincing or coherent. I will argue later, in chapter 4, that some of these theories (especially toward the extreme ends of the spectrum) are—in some cases despite their initial attractiveness—uninteresting or implausible. My concern in this chapter is to identify possible theories of democracy and to sort them into categories. I will hold my criticisms until later.

In chapter 3, I will return to my description of the behavioral approach to theories of democracy, and I will attempt to show some of the more important advantages of such an approach. Subsequently, in chapter 4, I will apply my behavioral approach to the theories of democracy presented here. Represented schematically, these theories appear in figure 1 (ranked from least epistemically demanding to most epistemically demanding).

(1999). In Przeworski's usage, the term applies to theories of democracy that have minimal expectations regarding likely products of democratic governments (e.g., their ability to generate socioeconomic equality). Although my use of the term will apply to some of the same theories of democracy (e.g., austere stability theories), my focus is on the kind of inputs required by the theories (i.e., reliable political judgment), rather than what they consider to be the likely products of democratic government.

[3] Joshua Cohen (1986) popularized the term "epistemic democracy" in dialogue with Coleman and Ferejohn (1986). His definition is instructive for us here, so I will quote it at length:

An epistemic interpretation of voting has three main elements: (1) an *independent standard* of correct decisions—that is, an account of justice or of the common good that is *independent* of current consensus and the outcome of votes; (2) a *cognitive* account of voting—that is, the view that voting expresses beliefs about what the correct policies are according to the independent standard, not personal preferences for policies; and (3) an account of *decision making* as a process of the adjustment of beliefs, adjustments that are undertaken in part in light of the evidence about the correct answer that is provided by the beliefs of others. Thus, the epistemic conception treats processes of decision making as, potentially, rational processes of the formation of common judgments. (34)

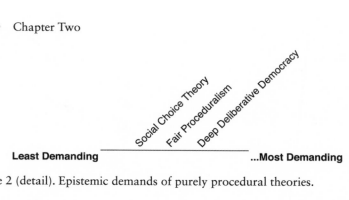

Figure 2 (detail). Epistemic demands of purely procedural theories.

2.1 PURELY PROCEDURAL THEORIES

One influential way of thinking about democracy involves claiming that it consists of a set of procedures that we find valuable for their own sake. Here, democratic procedures are considered intrinsically valuable and thus do not rely on any substantive claims about the correctness of political judgment: as long as these procedures are in place, democracy's value is assured, regardless of how individuals judge. Given the wide diversity of purely procedural theories of democracy, I will limit myself to a brief sketch of the most prominent forms: social choice theory, fair proceduralism, and deep deliberative democracy.[4] In each case, these theories claim that democratic procedures themselves, regardless of their outcomes, legitimate democratic government. As a result, they make only the most minimal epistemic demands of citizens.

2.1.1 Social Choice Theory

Social choice theory, popularized by Kenneth Arrow (Arrow 1951), seeks to understand democratic government in terms of the relationship that obtains between individual preferences and government policies within societies that carry out regular elections. This literature focuses on problems involved in aggregating individual preferences into a coherent and stable collective preference. For the most part, social choice theory is better understood as a set of criticisms of electoral arrangements[5] than

---

[4] Throughout this section, I draw heavily on David Estlund's recent work, especially his *Democratic Authority: A Philosophical Framework* (Estlund 2008). It should be noted that Estlund criticizes purely procedural theories, claiming that they must in the end admit procedure-independent standards for democratic decision making (i.e., he claims that they cannot remain *purely* procedural). For the time being, I will try to take these theories at face value, although I am sympathetic to Estlund's criticisms.

[5] For an interesting summary of these criticisms, see "Slinging Arrows at Democracy: Social Choice Theory, Value Pluralism, and Democratic Politics" (Pildes and Anderson

as an endorsement of democracy.[6] Since its publication, Arrow's impossibility theorem has been interpreted to recommend various nondemocratic political arrangements. Invoking Arrow, theorists have claimed that voting should be avoided in favor of free markets (Buchanan 1954), constitutions (Buchanan and Tullock 1962), and bureaucracies (Mashaw 1997).

As a result, theories of social choice have a vexed relationship with democracy. For my purposes here, it will suffice to point out that insofar as social choice theory manages to normatively endorse democracy, it does so on the basis of purely procedural values. In particular, theories of social choice recommend procedures that can successfully aggregate individual preferences in a way that allows them to influence government policies. Because the relationship between preferences and policies is not geared toward producing specific kinds of outcomes (e.g., good ones), social choice theory places very few epistemic demands on the judgment of citizens. Given that the grounds on which these theories endorse democracy are purely procedural, their endorsement is logically independent of concerns about the reliability of citizens' political judgments.[7]

2.1.2 Fair Proceduralism

Another popular account of democratic government maintains that democracy, and majority rule in particular, is justified because it is fair. That is, democracy represents a procedure for making decisions in such a way that no one's beliefs or interests count for more than anyone else's. On these accounts, democratic decision making is justified because it provides a way to make decisions in the face of widespread disagreement that does not provide anyone with an unfair influence over political decision making.[8] Like theories of social choice, fair proceduralism refuses to

---

1990). For an instructive analysis of the genesis of social choice theory and its critical orientation toward democracy, see *Democratic Devices and Desires* (Brennan and Hamlin 2000).

[6] William Riker's endorsement of a modest form of Madisonian liberalism (as opposed to Rousseauian populism) is the most influential endorsement of democracy grounded in the theoretical results of social choice (see J. Cohen 1986; Coleman and Ferejohn 1986; Pateman 1986). On Riker's view, the kind of democracy that survives critical scrutiny "is not, however, popular rule, but rather an intermittent, sometimes random, even perverse, popular veto" (Riker 1982a, 244). Unfortunately, it is not clear whether Riker's endorsement is thus purely procedural or more akin to a stability theory.

[7] There is a strand of this research, which I will call unorthodox social choice theory, that does indeed see a role for individual judgments about the collective good in democratic theory. See section 2.3.1.

[8] For an account of the relationship between political disagreement and democratic fairness, see Jeremy Waldron's *Law and Disagreement* (1999c). For an account that

apply external standards of evaluation (e.g., truth, prudence, or justice) to democratic decisions, emphasizing instead a formal feature of the procedure itself: it provides every voter with exactly the same amount of influence over democratic outcomes. In this way it too avoids placing any substantive demands on political judgment. Whether individuals make reliably good political decisions is irrelevant if all we care about is the procedural fairness of democracy.

2.1.3 Deep Deliberative Democracy

In recent years there has been an amazing proliferation of work on the topic of deliberative democracy.[9] This literature is increasingly diverse, but it is unified by a commitment to the value of rational deliberation in politics.[10] Deliberative theories claim that the use of coercive political power in democracies can be justified only if certain constraints on political procedures are satisfied. Although there is disagreement about the specifics of these constraints, most deliberative theorists agree that conditions of publicity, equality, and access must be met in order for democratic decisions to be legitimate.

There is a tension within theories of deliberative democracy, however, regarding the importance of deliberation. On some accounts deliberation is only intrinsically valuable: deliberative procedures are to be sought for their own sake, regardless of their effect on democratic outcomes. According to other theories, deliberation takes on an additional, instrumental value: deliberation is good because political decisions that are generated under conditions of deliberative publicity, equality, and accessibility are better than those that are not governed by these procedures. The former theories, which view deliberation as intrinsically valuable, are what I will call theories of deep deliberative democracy. The latter theories, which view deliberation as instrumentally valuable as well, are what I will call theories of epistemic deliberative democracy (see section 2.3.2).[11]

---

focuses on the role of publicity and equality, see Thomas Christiano's *The Constitution of Equality* (2008).

[9] There are a number of useful compilations of essays on deliberative democracy (Bohman and Rehg 1997; Elster 1998; Fishkin and Laslett 2003; van Aaken et al. 2004; Besson and Martí 2006). Canonical formulations of deliberative democracy are found in the work of Seyla Benhabib (1996), Joshua Cohen (1997, 2002), James Fishkin (1991), Samuel Freeman (2000), Jürgen Habermas (1996), as well as Amy Gutmann and Dennis Thompson (1996).

[10] For one novel variant, see the work of John Dryzek (Dryzek 2000, 2001; Dryzek and List 2003).

[11] For an instructive discussion of the different strands of deliberative theory, see David Estlund's Introduction to *Democracy* (Estlund 2002a, 1–27). I have also adapted the terms

Like other pure proceduralisms, deep deliberative democracy shuns procedure-independent standards for democratic decisions. Instead, these theories claim that the only standards applicable to democratic decisions are procedural: democratic decisions are legitimate if and only if they issue from the right procedures. In order to specify what these procedures might be, recourse is often made to the notion of an ideal deliberative procedure (J. Cohen 2002). Deep deliberative democrats claim that democratic decisions are legitimate if rational persons in an ideal deliberative setting could agree to the procedures governing those decisions.[12] In this way, it is the procedures, and not any characteristics of the outcomes themselves, that serve as the source of democratic legitimacy. As a result, deep theories of deliberative democracy place very few explicit demands on political judgment: proper deliberation is dependent on having the right procedures, not on correct political judgment.

2.2 STABILITY THEORIES

Another controversial set of democratic theories endorses democracy, not for the procedures that it embodies, but rather because of a specific outcome that it is expected to promote. This privileged democratic outcome consists in the ability of elections to produce stability. Stability theories endorse democracy because it provides a peaceful means of transitioning from one group of rulers to the next. Such theories rely on the empirically falsifiable claim that elections provide for a more stable means of transitioning between rulers than any other available form of government. On these views, democracy amounts to a kind of power-sharing arrangement among political elites that has the beneficial consequence of avoiding widespread violence or revolution.[13]

2.2.1 Austere Stability Theories

Even if we accept the stability theorists' claim that regular elections provide a peaceful method for transferring power between political elites, bloodless transitions between governments do not ensure anything about

---

"deep deliberative democracy" and "epistemic deliberative democracy" from Estlund's work (Estlund 2008).

[12] For complexities resulting from the locution "could agree," see chapter 2 of Hugh Baxter's *Habermas: The Discourse Theory of Law and Democracy* (2011).

[13] Joseph Schumpeter proposed an influential version of this view in his *Capitalism, Socialism, and Democracy* (1950).

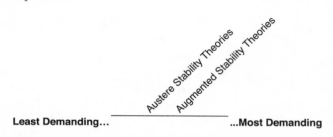

Figure 3 (detail). Epistemic demands of stability theories.

the quality of government that will obtain between elections. Theories that admit that democratic governments cannot be expected to make substantively good political decisions are what I will call austere stability theories. These theories endorse democracy for its ability to avoid the violence and social chaos that has traditionally accompanied the struggle for power between elite groups in nondemocratic societies. They do not, however, claim that democracy will generate good political outcomes over and above the social stability afforded by periodic elections. On this kind of view, democratic leaders will behave in ways that suit their own interests, and democratic government should not be expected to pursue the common good of society.

These are, it should be admitted, rather meager grounds on which to endorse democracy. It should be noted, however, that even to ensure this kind of stability, some demands on the judgment of citizens must be met. In particular, it must be the case that individuals in democratic societies will permit themselves to be ruled by the announced winners of elections (Przeworski 2003). This is not an insignificant demand, especially if it were widely agreed that the only normative grounds recommending democratic rule was the prevention of violence between political elites. Austere stability theories must rely on individuals judging it to be in their best interests to pursue the stability provided for by elections, rather than attempting to secure other political arrangements by nondemocratic means.

2.2.2 Augmented Stability Theories

In order to show that democracy can be relied on to produce more in terms of the quality of democratic rule, various additional claims have been made in behalf of stability theories of democracy. In general, these claims attempt to augment stability theories by building in modifications intended to show that democracy has more to offer than just stability.

Three augmentations are most important: competition, selection, and political freedom.[14]

2.2.2.1 COMPETITION

The existence of numerous groups of elites vying for political power provides for the possibility of competition among these groups for the opportunity to rule. Competition between these groups (construed on the model of market competition) will encourage elites—during campaigns and to a lesser degree while governing—to cater to the wishes of voters. This competition, it is argued, ensures a certain degree of responsiveness on the part of elites to the needs of the electorate. In order to gain a competitive advantage over other groups of elites, prospective rulers will attempt to gratify the desires of the electorate. This responsiveness, it is argued, may serve to raise the quality of political decisions in democracies. It should be noted, though, that in order for this responsiveness to lead to better decisions, it must be the case that adhering to voters' wishes will lead to good outcomes and that political elites are capable of being genuinely responsive to those wishes.

2.2.2.2 SELECTION

Another strategy for augmenting the justification of democracy provided by austere stability theories is to claim that competition for political office will lead to the selection of leaders with sound political judgment. As part of the democratic process, it is claimed, individuals possessing superior political judgment will be selected for positions of political power. In short, these theories claim that as a result of competition for political power, leaders can be relied on to make correct judgments. This requires that political competition in a democracy picks out those with good judgment rather than those with ambition, wealth, or power.

2.2.2.3 POLITICAL FREEDOM

One final augmentation to stability theories involves the claim that political elites, in order to see to it that electoral processes endure, must ensure the existence of a public forum within which political competition can take place. If competitive democracy is to survive, voters must be provided with a space in which they can voice their political opinions. This, it is argued, requires that leaders protect basic rights to freedom of speech and political participation. As a result, the existence of a limited set of political freedoms can be seen as a necessary constraint

---

[14] Augmentations such as these can be found in the work of Anthony Downs (1957), Gary Becker (1976), and Richard Posner (2003).

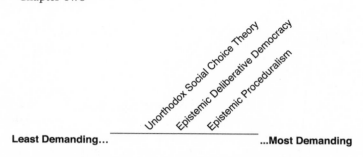

Least Demanding...   ...Most Demanding

Figure 4 (detail). Epistemic demands of modified procedural theories.

on stability theories of democracy. Political elites, then, must at the very least have enough good judgment to ensure that these freedoms are protected.

2.3 Modified Procedural Theories

In the past ten years there has emerged a number of hybrid theories of democracy that seek to combine elements of both procedural and epistemic accounts of democratic government. I call them modified procedural theories, because they can be usefully interpreted as building epistemic claims into a proceduralist justification of democracy. Three variants will be considered here: unorthodox social choice theory, epistemic deliberative democracy, and epistemic proceduralism.

2.3.1 Unorthodox Social Choice Theory

As we have seen, social choice theory denies the existence of independent standards for the evaluation of democratic outcomes. It focuses on the formal relationship between individual preferences and government policies. In its orthodox form, social choice theory is thus purely procedural: it sees democracy's value (insofar as it is seen to be valuable) as a function of electoral procedures and not democratic outcomes. Recently, however, a strand of social choice has emerged that proposes a new role for individual judgment within democracies.[15] Unorthodox social choice theory, as I will call it, combines the tools of social choice with an expressive theory of voting in order to propose a series of institutional reforms

[15] Geoffrey Brennan has developed this view in conjunction with various coauthors. In particular, see *Democracy and Decision: The Pure Theory of Electoral Preference* (Brennan and Lomasky 1993), *Democratic Devices and Desires* (Brennan and Hamlin 2000), and *The Economy of Esteem: An Essay on Civil and Political Society* (Brennan and Pettit 2004).

geared toward promoting the efficacy of moral motivations in the political realm.[16] It recognizes the existence of the public interest in politics and argues that democratic institutions ought to be designed in such a way as to mobilize the moral motivations of citizens in order to promote it.[17]

This is a complicated normative view, but what is important for my purposes is the manner in which it combines procedural concerns about government responsiveness to citizens' preferences with a novel account of democratic voting. As a result of certain features of large-scale elections, the expressed preferences of citizens (their votes) are expected to reflect their considered moral judgment about political questions rather than their narrow self-interest.[18] If this is the case, then a procedural concern for government responsiveness will require the aggregation of individual moral judgments about politics. If these judgments are accurate, then democratic government can and should be expected to promote the common good.

Unorthodox social choice theory is interesting because it combines a procedural justification of democracy (government policies should reflect individual preferences) with a theory of institutional design geared toward making moral judgments about the public interest politically efficacious. Insofar as unorthodox social choice theory demands not only that democracy be responsive to expressed preferences, but also promote the collective good, it must partially embrace an epistemic theory of democracy: making good judgments in politics is part of the proper function of democratic government. To the extent that this is the case, unorthodox social choice theory must make substantive demands on the political judgment of citizens in a democracy. For it is only if individual political judgments are accurate that institutional mechanisms can be deployed to secure the public interest.

---

[16] The theory of expressive voting claims that voters cast their ballots in ways that make themselves feel good about their political and moral views, rather than attempting to secure particular electoral outcomes.

[17] Brennan and Lomasky focus on voter morality, electoral institutions, and constitutions (Brennan and Lomasky 1993, 2000). Brennan and Hamlin consider elections, representation, political parties, and the separation of powers (Brennan and Hamlin 2000, 2002). Brennan and Pettit examine the iron hand of the state, the invisible hand of the market, and the intangible hand of esteem (Brennan and Pettit 1993, 2004).

[18] Most important, this view holds that individual voters have such a small likelihood of being decisive with regard to the outcome (the chance of casting the tie-breaking vote in most large-scale elections is negligible) that the relative cost of expressing their moral opinion on pressing political issues is low enough to encourage them to register their moral judgment on the issue at hand, rather than merely indicating which of the outcomes is in their own interest (Brennan 1989). For two accounts that also accept the inefficacy of voting but arrive at very different conclusions, see Russell Hardin's *How Do You Know?* (2009) and Jason Brennan's *The Ethics of Voting* (2011).

2.3.2 Epistemic Deliberative Democracy

As we saw above, there are two strands of deliberative democracy: one deeply procedural and the other epistemic. Whereas the procedural strand views deliberation as only intrinsically valuable, the epistemic variant construes deliberation as both instrumentally and intrinsically valuable. Epistemic deliberative theories claim that public deliberation among citizens leads to good political decisions, where these decisions are measured against a procedure-independent standard of correctness.[19] Epistemic deliberative theories would thus seem to put very exacting demands on the reliability of deliberative groups, but for the most part they avoid making the value of deliberation entirely dependent on its epistemic value. Instead, epistemic deliberative theories tie deliberation both to a tendency to make correct political judgments and to the legitimacy (or authority) of government (Estlund 1997b; Gaus 1997b; Martí 2006).

Citizens' judgments must be accurate in order to enable good democratic decisions, and the institutions governing deliberation must be effective in order to ensure that deliberation can improve this decision making, but for deliberative epistemic theories such concerns are only part of the justification of democratic rule.[20] Deliberation, on this view, provides both epistemic value and legitimacy to democratic government. As a result, the cognitive demands on epistemic theories of democracy are tempered by procedural concerns regarding legitimacy. Because the procedural legitimacy of deliberation does not impose any cognitive demands on the judgment of citizens, epistemic deliberative theories take a moderate stance on epistemic reliability: epistemic value is part of the justification of democracy but so is legitimacy, and as these two qualities are logically independent of one another, there will be cases where democratic judgment should be traded off in favor of procedural legitimacy.

2.3.3 Epistemic Proceduralism

David Estlund proposes a version of modified proceduralism that is in some ways similar to epistemic deliberative democracy. Like epistemic deliberative theories, Estlund seeks to incorporate concerns about epistemic value into a theory that places procedural constraints on legitimacy and authority. The manner in which he does so, however, is importantly different from the views we examined above.

---

[19] For an interesting defense of this view, see "The Epistemic Conception of Deliberative Democracy Defended: Reasons, Rightness and Equal Political Autonomy" (Martí 2006). See also *The Constitution of Deliberative Democracy* (Nino 1996).

[20] Recently, empirical concerns have been raised about the effect of deliberation on political preferences (Sunstein 2000b; Lupia 2002; Druckman and Nelson 2003).

Estlund's epistemic proceduralism claims that the authority and legitimacy of democratic government derives from the fact that it is the epistemically best political arrangement that meets with what he calls "general acceptability." That is, he claims that democracy does the best job of tracking the truth of all political arrangements that can be agreed to in light of certain constraints on political justification.[21] He states: "Democratically produced laws are legitimate and authoritative because they are produced by a procedure with a tendency to make correct decisions. It is not an infallible procedure, and there might even be more accurate procedures. But democracy is better than random and the epistemically best among those that are generally acceptable in the way that political legitimacy requires" (Estlund 2008, 8).

As a result, Estlund's epistemic proceduralism is more dependent on the reliability of individual judgments than are epistemic theories of deliberative democracy. Because, for him, the authority and legitimacy of democracy is dependent (at least in part) on its value as a tracker of truth, his entire justification of democracy would be undermined if citizens were unable to meet the epistemic burdens set by his theory. Whereas for epistemic deliberativists, epistemic value and legitimacy constitute two independent concerns, for Estlund they are inseparable (i.e., some degree of epistemic reliability is necessary for the legitimacy of democratic decisions). That said, epistemic proceduralism requires that democracy possess only a moderate epistemic value, as it does not need to be the best possible decision-making arrangement, but merely the best from among those that are generally acceptable. In this way, Estlund's theory makes fewer epistemic demands than conventional epistemic theories of democracy.

2.4 Epistemic Theories

The most demanding theories of democracy are what I call epistemic theories of democracy. These theories tie democracy's proper function directly to its ability to generate substantively correct political judgments. There are a number of interesting variations of epistemic theories of democracy, but I will here focus on just three. Epistemic theories of democracy either justify democracy on the basis of explicitly epistemic norms (dialogical democracy), require that democracy provide a reliable

---

[21] In this respect, epistemic proceduralism relies on a version of Rawls's liberal principle of legitimacy (Rawls 1993). On this issue, see David Estlund, "Making Truth Safe for Democracy" (1995) and David Copp, "Could Political Truth Be a Hazard for Democracy?" (1995), as well as "The Insularity of the Reasonable: Why Political Liberalism Must Admit the Truth" (Estlund 1998).

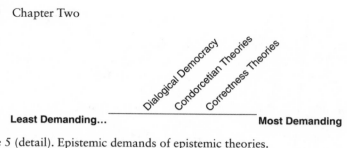

Figure 5 (detail). Epistemic demands of epistemic theories.

guide to the common good (Condorcetian theories), or claim that democratic government is only legitimate when it yields correct political decisions (correctness theories).

2.4.1 Dialogical Democracy

Robert Talisse has recently argued for a justification of democracy that is distinctive because of its rejection of moral principles as the appropriate ground of democracy's value.[22] Talisse rejects the common presumption that the justification of democracy must rely on collectively held moral principles, arguing instead for an epistemological justification of democracy.[23] He claims that democracy's value stems from our individual commitment to holding true beliefs. According to Talisse, part of what it means to have beliefs is that one is committed to a series of epistemological principles that can only be satisfied within a democratic social order. He thus justifies democracy on the basis of implicit assumptions of our "folk epistemology":[24] "[O]nly in a democracy can an individual practice proper epistemic agency; put in other words, only in a democracy can one be a proper believer. Since we are already committed to proper believing, we are implicitly committed to democratic politics" (Talisse 2009a, 121).

This justification of democracy makes significant demands on the judgment of citizens. Indeed, Talisse argues that dialogical democracy requires what he calls an "epistemically perfectionist state" (Talisse 2009a, p. 156). On this account, in order for democracy to be valuable, citizens must have the whole set of communicative, formal, informational, methodological, and interpersonal capabilities necessary for epistemic agency (Talisse 2009a, p. 175). It should be noted, however, that this does not commit Talisse to the view that in order to be justified, a democracy must ensure that no one has any false beliefs. Instead, he seems to be

[22] See *Democracy and Moral Conflict* (2009a) as well as "An Epistemological Defense of Democracy" (2010).

[23] For a clear example of the sort of view Talisse is rejecting, see Ronald Dworkin's *Is Democracy Possible Here?* (2006a).

[24] See also Talisse (2009b, 2010).

committed to the view that democracy is justified if it provides everyone with these epistemic capabilities up to a certain (unspecified) threshold.[25] This is an exacting standard, to be sure, but it falls short of the demands of the most epistemic theories of democracy.

2.4.2 Condorcetian Theories

In the eighteenth century, Marie Jean Antoine Nicolas Caritat, better known as the Marquis de Condorcet, proposed a mathematical theorem designed to establish the reliability of decision making by large juries (Condorcet 1976). More recently, Condorcet's jury theorem has been interpreted to establish an epistemic argument in favor of democratic government.[26] It asserts that if we aggregate the decisions of a group whose members are more likely than not to get the right answer to a given question, then the overall reliability of the group increases as we expand its members. It implies that if voters have better-than-random individual competences, then large democratic groups will have a very high group competence. Condorcet's jury theorem thus provides a straightforward epistemic argument supporting democratic government: when certain conditions are met, democracy (understood as majority rule) will provide a highly reliable political decision-making procedure.[27]

As a result, epistemic theories of democracy grounded in Condorcet's jury theorem—which I call Condorcetian theories of democracy—will demand quite a bit from citizens. These theories require that, on average, citizens in a democracy will possess political judgment that is at least better than random. Failing that, the theorem spells disaster for democratic decision making: if citizens are more likely than not to get the wrong answers to political questions, then decision making in large democracies is almost certain to go astray every time (Goodin and Estlund 2004). Notice, however, that Condorcetian theories need not require that

[25] Here Talisse models his account on Martha Nussbaum's capabilities approach. See Nussbaum (2000, 2007).

[26] Condorcet's jury theorem was ushered into democratic theory with the help of Duncan Black (1958) and Brian Barry (1965). Since then, this theorem has been highly influential (Estlund 1994; List and Goodin 2001; Bovens and Rabinowicz 2004; Goodin and Estlund 2004; List and Pettit 2011), with a great deal written about the relationship between Rousseau and Condorcet (Levine 1976; Weirich 1986; Grofman and Feld 1988; Estlund et al. 1989; Waldron 1993b).

[27] These conditions include, but are not limited to, the requirement that individuals in the group have an average competence that is better than random (Goodin and Estlund 2004). In addition, it requires that voter's decisions be independent from one another (Estlund 1994). Until recently, the theorem's application was restricted to choices between two options, but it has now been generalized to many-optioned choices as well (List and Goodin 2001).

individual competence is better than random on every political issue, only that on average it is better than mere chance. As a result, a Condorcetian theory of democracy can turn a blind eye to some failings in the judgment of citizens (e.g., if our judgment fails regarding some of the more arcane issues in tax policy), as long as—across the whole spectrum of political questions—we are more likely than not to get the correct answer.

2.4.3 Correctness Theories

Perhaps the most radical kind of demand that could be placed on our political judgment by a theory of democracy consists in the requirement that in order to be legitimate, political decisions must be correct. That is, one could insist that political judgments are legitimate if and only if they meet independent standards of correctness.[28] On such an account, democratic legitimacy is dependent on the accuracy of our collective political judgments. Here, the proper function of government is to get the right answer to political questions: insofar as democracy does that, it is legitimate, but if it fails to do so, it is illegitimate. Of all theories of democracy, therefore, correctness theories place the most stringent demands on the reliability of citizens' judgment.

2.5 CONCLUSION

As we can now see, there is an enormous range of epistemic demands placed on political judgment by different theories of democracy. As a result, one's assessment of the relevance of framing effects to democratic theory will depend very heavily on what kind of democratic theory one endorses. In the following chapter, I will examine how a behavioral approach to democratic theory understands the relevance of empirical evidence regarding the judgment of citizens. Then, in chapter 4, I will use this approach to assess the significance of framing effects for the categories of democratic theory described above.

---

[28] Such an account has been attributed to Rousseau (Estlund 1997a), though there are several complications regarding his democratic theory (Gaus 1997a).

CHAPTER THREE

Behavioral Democratic Theory

IN THIS CHAPTER, I lay out the advantages of a behavioral approach to democratic theory. In particular, I contrast this approach with three more common ways of treating the decision making of citizens in a democracy. In order to bring out the contrast, I use the notion of epistemic competence to stand in for the various cognitive skills and abilities that are required for democracy to function properly. I show that rejecting the rational actor model of human decision making allows us to focus on three important theoretical considerations. First, the behavioral approach facilitates the use of a cost-benefit analysis regarding the proposed advantages of democracy. This allows us to examine more clearly the appropriate moral reasons for endorsing democratic government. Second, it enables us to see more readily what practical limitations are associated with particular theories of democracy. This permits us to focus on the feasibility of particular theories of democracy in a way that is not possible under different approaches. Third, and most important for my purposes, the behavioral approach to normative democratic theory forces us to consider the implications for institutional design of different theories of democracy.

This chapter proceeds in three stages. First, I propose the notion of epistemic competence as a way to simplify discussion of the empirical data relevant to my account. Next, I consider and reject three familiar approaches to democratic theory. Finally, I explain the benefits of a behavioral approach to normative theories of democracy.

3.1 EMPIRICAL DATA AND NORMATIVE DEMOCRATIC THEORY

There is an enormous amount of empirical information that might be relevant for our theorizing about democratic government: facts about the economic status of citizens, facts about their moral and political doctrines, and even facts about existing relationships with other nations or states might all be relevant to our understanding of how (and whether) democracies will function. Even if we restrict ourselves to considering the judgment of individual citizens, there is still a startling array of information that might be relevant to our assessment of democracy. Data about citizens' moral judgment, their skills of inference, and their emotional reactions are all relevant to an assessment of the reliability of individual political judgment. In this chapter, I would like to speak in a general way about the kind of political judgment required by democracy. In order to do this, I will use the notion of "epistemic competence" to stand in for a whole range of individual skills and abilities. In this way, I will briefly expand my focus from the phenomenon of framing effects to political judgment conceived more broadly. I do this in order to highlight the appeal of a behavioral approach to democratic theory. In chapter 4, I will once again narrow my focus and bring the behavioral approach developed here to bear on the particular theories of democracy described in chapter 2.

3.1.1 Epistemic Competence

My concern in this chapter will be the "epistemic competence" of citizens: the judgmental capacities required of them in their role as voters.[1] The epistemic capacities I have in mind include the talents and skills, powers and abilities that are put to use in citizens' judgments and decisions about politics. These capacities are epistemic in that they underwrite the political knowledge of citizens. It is important to note, however, that these capacities do not themselves constitute knowledge of politics: I am not going to discuss the information that citizens have (or do not have) concerning politics, but rather the capacities that allow them to make use of the information they do have.[2]

In using the term "competence," I follow others in claiming that competence is best understood as a threshold concept (in contrast with a comparative one).[3] That is to say that calling someone "competent" is to claim that his or her abilities surpass some standard (this requires, in

[1] I should note that in focusing on the capacities required to make correct judgments about political issues, I exclude from my consideration the moral capacities that may be required of citizens in a democracy. There may be reason to wonder also whether citizens have the moral capacities required by democratic government (Kinder and Kiewiet 1981; Caplan 2002), but I cannot address these questions here. I am interested in whether, if citizens wanted to, they could meet the epistemic demands of democratic citizenship.

[2] It might be objected that recent work in virtue epistemology (Fairweather and Zagzebski 2001; BonJour and Sosa 2003) has called into question the distinction between intellectual and ethical virtue (Zagzebski 1996, 2003). If it is the case that epistemic capacities are ultimately indistinguishable from moral capacities, then failures of political judgment will involve the violation of moral as well as epistemic norms. Although this would be a surprising implication, it does not appear to be hostile to the arguments sketched here. I thank Iskra Fileva for calling my attention to this issue.

[3] The literature concerning competence in medical ethics has been particularly instructive here. The decision-relative concept of competence developed by Dan Brock and Allen Buchanan (Brock and Buchanan 1986; Buchanan and Brock 1989) provides the framework for my construal of epistemic competence in this section. The similarities and differences

the present context, giving up the temptation to use locutions like "she's more competent than he"). Notice, however, that I do not intend to specify what standard constitutes epistemic competence in a democracy. This would be counterproductive here, as it would restrict us to the discussion of a particular theory of democracy. Instead, I want to stipulate that the standard of competence will vary with the theory of democracy that one favors, and I propose to let each theory determine competence by its own lights. Some theories will have highly demanding standards of epistemic competence; others will have only minimal ones.

Determining whether or not we are epistemically competent thus involves determining where we fall on a spectrum of epistemic abilities. In particular, epistemic competence requires that we rank above a certain threshold. This threshold specifies what kind of epistemic abilities are required for democratic governments to function properly. Notice also that I don't intend to specify what it means for a democracy to function properly. Again, this is not appropriate here, as different theories of democracy specify different standards for proper democratic functioning. As a result, I propose to let theories of democracy determine both what is required for proper functioning (i.e., what epistemic threshold must be met) and what constitutes proper function itself (e.g., what functions democratic governments are expected to fulfill). In this way, we can speak in general terms about the epistemic demands placed on citizens without constraining the discussion to a particular theory of democracy.

3.2 THREE APPROACHES

Currently, however, most normative theories of democracy do not attempt to incorporate empirical data regarding epistemic competence. Instead, three alternative strategies predominate: (1) the factual assertion, (2) the idealizing assumption, and (3) the moral principle. In this section, I propose and evaluate these approaches and explain how they treat the epistemic competence of citizens. Although I acknowledge certain limited cases where these three strategies might be acceptable, I think that the discipline of normative democratic theory should pursue another course. More specifically, I argue that none of the strategies outlined here manage to successfully arbitrate between normative and empirical concerns relevant to democratic theory. In order to engage satisfactorily with both descriptive evidence and moral values, normative democratic theory must

---

between the role of competence in these two areas—medicine and politics—merits serious further study.

be capable of responding to facts about the world in a manner that none of these three approaches manages to achieve. This is what distinguishes the behavioral approach to normative democratic theory.

3.2.1 The Factual Assertion

The most obvious, and perhaps most common, way of addressing the competence of citizens is simply to assert that individuals have the requisite skills and abilities required for the proper function of democratic government. Here, normative theories of democracy treat it as uncontroversial that citizens will have the epistemic capacities demanded by democracy.

This approach is familiar largely as a result of the adoption in democratic theory of the model of human decision making traditionally employed in economics. The rational actor model of human decision making views individuals as utility maximizers who effectively manage their decisions so as to secure their interests. Following this model, many theories of democracy simply assert that individuals make political judgments (e.g., vote) in ways that effectively serve their interests.[4] Even theories that do not explicitly adopt the perspective of traditional economics often assume that citizens will display an unbounded rationality in their judgments about politics (e.g., they don't make mistakes about their own interests, they accurately predict prospects for the future, and they accurately represent the implications of their own beliefs). In this way, the factual assertion of competence has given the rational actor model of human decision making a firm foothold in normative democratic theory.

However, if we assert—as a matter of fact—that people have the epistemic capacities required for the proper functioning of democracy, then we open ourselves up to the possible empirical falsification of this claim. Because I have chosen to construe competence as a threshold concept, where the threshold is determined elsewhere, it is important to note that the factual assertion that citizens are competent will have varying degrees of plausibility depending on the threshold. Theories of democracy that require very little of citizens by way of epistemic ability ought therefore to enjoy more factual plausibility than those that demand more. However, all but the most minimalist theories involve substantial assumptions about the epistemic abilities of citizens.[5] Thus, only a small number of

---

[4] This is particularly evident among economic theories of democracy (Downs 1957) and theories of social choice (Arrow 1951; Buchanan and Tullock 1962).

[5] A purely procedural theory that makes no demands on citizens' judgment would count as an example of a theory of democracy that places the threshold for epistemic competence so low (the capacity to merely register a vote) as to avoid any empirical challenge regarding our actual epistemic abilities.

democratic theories can avoid making claims about competence that are controversial on empirical grounds.

Just as other disciplines have had to deal with empirical challenges to the rationality of individual judgments, so should democratic theory: we must consider the mounting empirical evidence that the rational actor model of human decision making is simply not an accurate description of our actual behavior. For the majority of democratic theories, the problem with this model is the existence of disturbing empirical research that describes serious problems in our decision making. The most influential research relevant here is the heuristics and biases literature.[6] These results, though discouraging, do not reveal that human decision making is completely unreliable.[7] Instead, the picture revealed by this literature is a complicated mixture of cognitive successes and failures.[8] Thus, whether or not citizens are epistemically competent will be largely determined by where we set the bar. Our epistemic abilities seem to be rather middling: we demonstrate a whole range of quirks and foibles, but there are certain tasks that we perform well enough, at least most of the time. As a result, if our favored democratic theory sets the threshold for competence low enough, then psychologists might deem us competent. If, however, we endorse a particularly demanding theory of democracy, then the heuristics and biases literature might cast doubt on our status as competent citizens.

Thus, in order to pursue the strategy of asserting that citizens are competent to serve the purposes of democracy, democratic theorists would have to argue, on empirical grounds, that the actual cognitive capacities of citizens surpass whatever epistemic standard they specify. This sort of empirical debate is not common among political philosophers or political theorists. Anyone who wants to contend, as a factual matter, that citizens' epistemic capacities are accurate enough (for their favored theory of democracy) will need to engage psychologists, political scientists, and economists on their own turf, arguing empirical points with evidence

---

[6] This research includes, but is not exhausted by, the study of framing effects. For wider accounts of the pathologies that affect human decision making, see *How We Know What Isn't So* (Gilovich 1991), *Inevitable Illusions: How Mistakes of Reason Rule Our Minds* (Piattelli-Palmarini 1994), and the work of Jonathan Baron (1985, 2001, 2005, 2008).

[7] In fact, the use of cognitive heuristics has helped to explain a puzzle that has endured since Philip Converse's early studies (1964) of the American voter: given how little citizens appear to know about politics, how is it possible that democracies have continued to function at all? The fact that human decision making makes use of low-information cognitive shortcuts goes some way in explaining how serious information deficiencies might be counteracted by the use of heuristics (Popkin 1991).

[8] For an account that emphasizes these successes rather than the failures, see the work of Gerd Gigerenzer (Gigerenzer 1991; Gigerenzer, Todd, et al. 1999; Gigerenzer 2000; Gigerenzer and Selten 2001; Gigerenzer 2005; Gigerenzer and Engel 2006; Gigerenzer 2007).

and data. If the question of competence is treated merely as a matter of correctly determining the current state of our epistemic abilities, then normative democratic theorists ought to be willing to engage in these empirical debates in order to establish their claims.

This, however, is not an appealing prospect for most political philosophers. The desirability of democratic government is not usually treated as so radically contingent a matter: most theories of democracy view the value of democratic government as something at least prima facie impervious to empirical falsification. Thus, political philosophers stress that theirs are normative theories of democracy, not descriptive ones.[9] Many political philosophers discount the empirical data regarding competence because of the moral orientation of their discipline: the current state of civic competence is not taken to be relevant to how citizens ought to govern themselves. As a result, some political philosophers are content to simply ignore empirical data that testifies to low levels of epistemic reliability among citizens.

Unfortunately, most theories of democracy are premised on the existence of a reliable, competent citizenry responsible for ensuring, in one way or another, the proper functioning of democratic government.[10] Any theory of democracy that places epistemic demands on the abilities of citizens must acknowledge the possibility that actual citizens do not possess the capacities required by their theory. As a result, any argument in favor of such a theory of democracy must make empirical claims about epistemic competence. Because these claims are empirical, we ought to be willing to countenance the possibility that evidence from psychology or political science might militate against our favored theory of democracy. Whether or not, in fact, the evidence emerging from these disciplines actually undermines a given theory of democracy will be a complicated matter that I cannot address here.[11] However, insisting on the irrelevance of empirical data for normative democratic theory is unsustainable for any account of democracy that places epistemic demands on the deliberations, inferences, judgments, or decisions of citizens.

---

[9] For a particularly forceful articulation of the normative goals of political philosophy, see David Estlund's account of "Utopophobia" in *Democratic Authority* (Estlund 2008, chap. 14).

[10] Again, some purely procedural theories of democracy present a possible exception to this claim. For example, social choice theorists who specify the task of democracy merely in terms of government responsiveness to expressed voter preferences might be able to avoid placing epistemic demands on citizens. However, if such theories do not place any epistemic demands on voters, they cannot expect that democratic decisions will respect norms of prudence, rationality, or justice.

[11] In chapter 4, I will go some distance toward this end, as I explain how evidence of framing effects ought to influence particular theories of democracy.

3.2.2 The Idealizing Assumption

A different approach to democratic theory involves making use of competence as an idealizing assumption.[12] Here, the idea is to assume that citizens are competent in order to help approximate an ideal state of affairs, which can then be used to generate an account of justice, legitimacy, or authority.[13] In this way, competence is treated in the manner of many other political constraints. For instance, it is often the case that political philosophers make use of simplifying assumptions about the relative scarcity of resources, rates of compliance with the law, relations between states, and even the psychological makeup of persons. In each of these instances, we make assumptions that attempt to describe a possible state of affairs that is normatively superior to our own in order to ground conclusions about what ought to be the case. By assuming that citizens are competent, political philosophers describe an idealized world that then can be used to ground claims about the apposite nature or function of democratic government.

If the status of these assumptions is not made clear, however, it can often appear as though arguments that engage in this kind of ideal theory simply rest on false premises. As a result, many people outside of political philosophy simply dismiss such arguments as being unsound or as relying on an empirically unsupportable model of decision making. For this reason, empirical evidence that calls into question the epistemic competence of citizens has led some to dismiss the conclusions of this sort of ideal theory.

Such misunderstandings aside, there is a deeper problem with the use of idealizing assumptions in normative democratic theory. Many of us expect normative theories of democracy to provide us with guidance as to what kind of policies and activities are appropriate within our own societies. For instance, many of us look to normative democratic theory in order to determine whether or not we should support greater political participation by means of referendums and the like, whether we should support or oppose institutions like judicial review, and whether we should be worried about civic apathy and low voter turnout. If normative democratic theory makes use of idealizing assumptions about epistemic competence, it isn't clear that it can provide us with any guidance on these issues. Surely, it can describe a democratic ideal that is supposed to help

---

[12] The project of ideal theory was most influentially described by John Rawls in *Political Liberalism* (1993) and *The Law of Peoples* (1999a).

[13] I take Rawls, Habermas, and Estlund to be engaging in this kind of project in *A Theory of Justice* (Rawls 1999b), *Between Facts and Norms* (Habermas 1996), and *Democratic Authority* (Estlund 2008), respectively.

orient our thinking about such issues, but it is difficult to see how it can perform this orienting function.

The difficulty in relating an ideal theory to nonideal circumstances is especially pressing in the case of competence. Precisely because competence is a threshold concept, if the idealizing assumption does not hold in the actual world (if citizens fail to meet the epistemic standard of what is required of them in order for a democracy to function properly), then the results could be quite dire.[14] It is not at all clear then what practical implications we can derive from an ideal theory of democracy. This, it seems to me, is quite a disappointment for normative democratic theory. Although I think ideal theorizing about politics is important, it seems that if we are going to find serious thinking about what we actually ought to do in a democracy, we ought to find it in normative democratic theory. As long as competence is treated only as an idealizing assumption, however, we will not find any such guidance.

3.2.3 The Moral Principle

A third approach to the issue of competence in normative democratic theory is to link competence to some kind of moral principle. That is, we might claim that we are morally required to treat citizens as though they meet a given standard of competence, even if they in fact do not. In this way, there is no factual claim being made, nor is there any kind of simplifying assumption at play; instead it is asserted that citizens in a democracy ought to treat one another with a specific kind of mutual respect for their epistemic abilities. In this way, competence might be connected to other moral principles: to some version of a principle of equality or even to a principle of autonomy. In either case, we might try to derive the moral claim that citizens be treated as though they were competent from some more widely accepted principle.

Although construing competence in this way is attractive in its own right, I can think of no justification for doing so that does not appear ad hoc. Clearly it would be nice if we could ground competence in an uncontroversial moral principle, but this does not seem to be independently warranted. We might try to base treating people as though they were competent in a principle of equality, but that would require assuming (1) that some citizens are politically competent, and (2) that the appropriate way to treat everyone else is as though they were competent as

---

[14] As an example, we might recall what Condorcet's jury theorem indicates will be the case if citizens fall below the threshold of better-than-random decision making (Goodin and Estlund 2004). Here, the theorem predicts that large democracies will almost inevitably make systematically wrong choices. This is a particularly vivid example of what is called the theory of the second best in economics (Lipsey and Lancaster 1956).

well, rather than deciding to treat those competent persons as incompetent (which would also satisfy equality). Alternatively, we might try to claim that we must treat people as though they were competent in order to respect their autonomy, but using this principle requires that we adopt something like a Kantian view of persons in politics. Given that it is precisely this sort of picture of human cognitive abilities that has been challenged by the behavioral literature, we would need to provide a very compelling argument for using the principle of autonomy to ground claims about epistemic competence.

The most obvious way to ground this claim would be to tie it to the beneficial consequences of its adoption: if the effects of treating individuals as though they were competent were good enough, then these consequences might warrant the adoption of a moral principle requiring us to treat everyone in this way. Unfortunately, we don't yet have an argument that can establish that these good consequences would come to pass in a democracy, if it is not the case that people really are competent. In the absence of an independent argument for these consequences, I cannot see how we can ground the claim that we should be treated as though we were competent in a moral principle.[15]

3.3 Advantages of the Behavioral Approach

I should acknowledge that in the foregoing I have identified a number of cases in which the role of claims about competence should be clear and relatively unproblematic. First, some minimalist theories of democracy may demand so little of democratic government that their assertion that citizens are competent shouldn't be controversial. If such a theory sets the standard of competence low enough (say, at the level of merely being able to cast a vote), then asserting competence as a matter of fact would probably be above empirical reproach. Second, those interested in

---

[15] Historical arguments for democratic egalitarianism are importantly different from the consequentialist justification alluded to here. In the United States, for example, literacy tests and other attempts to restrict the franchise have been motivated primarily by racism and prejudice, and have had abysmal historical effects. Although this surely suffices to rule out such measures within a democracy, it does not address the theoretical question posed here. Historical evidence of the above sort demonstrates that democratic suffrage ought to be universal, but it doesn't show—even if we extend the franchise universally—that citizens have the epistemic capacities required for democracy to function properly. A democracy with universal suffrage is certainly going to have a better chance of meeting the epistemic requirements of democracy than one with literacy tests (or other such arbitrary restrictions), but this is not sufficient to show that treating us all collectively as though we were competent will yield the goods that democracy is taken (by particular theories of democracy) to offer.

constructing an ideal theory of democracy are entitled to make use of an idealizing assumption in order to dispense with the issue of competence. Although I applaud such theories in their own right, I think that we ought to expect more from normative democratic theory. Finally, I have to leave open the possibility that competence can be connected to an uncontroversial moral principle. If this were the case, then it might be possible to demand—morally—that we be treated as though we were competent, even if in fact we are not.

Leaving these cases aside, however, I think we should be dissatisfied with the role that competence currently plays in normative democratic theory. The prevailing conclusion of empirical social scientists seems to be that the epistemic capacities of citizens are significantly less reliable than has been presumed by most normative theorists.[16] This seems relevant for democratic theory. As a result, political philosophers ought to be in some way responsive to these empirical claims. To the extent that they are not, then I think that democratic theory, as a theoretical enterprise, suffers.

In order to rectify this oversight, I propose that we reject the strategies outlined above and instead adopt a behavioral approach to democracy. That is, I think we should consider the epistemic competence of citizens in light of the best available evidence from empirical social science. The behavioral approach is distinguished from other methods in democratic theory primarily for the manner in which it construes the relevance of this empirical research. Two points should be emphasized here. First, a behavioral approach to democratic theory rejects the rational actor model of human decision making and replaces that model with a more empirically accurate picture of human decision making. In this way, behavioral democratic theory must rely on the picture of human decision making and judgment that emerges from empirical psychology and the social sciences.[17] Second, in order to retain its credentials as a normative enterprise, the behavioral approach cannot construe competence as merely a matter of correctly describing current states of affairs.[18] A behavioral

[16] There is a wide range of evidence that could be cited here. My focus has been, and will continue to be, on data collected in the heuristics and biases literature (Kahneman, Slovic, et al. 1982; Kahneman and Tversky 2000c; Gilovich et al. 2002). Evidence of the confused and often contradictory political beliefs of American voters (Converse 1964; Converse et al. 1964; Converse 1970; Delli Carpini and Keeter 1996; Caplan 2008; Somin 2010) and of problems affecting group deliberation (Sunstein 2000b, 2006) is also relevant.

[17] Currently, the most well-developed and convincing model of human judgment is proposed by the heuristics and biases literature. This, however, is a contingent matter, and it may eventually be the case that another empirical model of human decision making ought to be employed in behavioral democratic theory.

[18] There is a tension here between these two points. Theorizing of the sort that I propose must avoid making strong idealizing assumptions in order to engage with empirical

approach to democratic theory thus recognizes that competence is tied to moral concerns about the proper function and value of democratic government. As a result, behavioral democratic theory cannot be content with merely ascertaining whether citizens in fact have the capacities required by a given theory of democracy, but rather, it must evaluate competence always in light of the relevant moral considerations.[19]

In the sections that follow, I describe three particular advantages that behavioral democratic theory has over the approaches discussed above. These advantages include moral, practical, and institutional considerations.

3.3.1 Moral Reasons

One upshot of abandoning the rational actor model of human decision making is that doing so requires us to be clear about the moral importance of claims about competence. Given that, on the behavioral approach, we are not entitled to assume that citizens have the epistemic capacities required for the function of democratic government, we must be willing to explain why it is that we are entitled to demand that individuals gain or possess these capacities. In this way, the behavioral approach requires us to be clearer about the moral reasons for endorsing democratic government: insofar as competence comes at a cost, we should be willing to explain what moral reasons there are for incurring this cost.

It should be apparent that the burden we ought to be willing to bear in order to attain a certain standard of competence is dependent on the goods we hope will accrue to a democracy composed of competent citizens. There might be very strong moral reasons to gain competence or there might only be rather weak reasons. The strength of the moral reasons in favor of attaining a competent citizenry will depend on what theory of democracy we are evaluating. Although theories of democracy differ regarding the moral reasons for endorsing democracy, some of the mainstays of what they claim a properly functioning democracy has to

---

research. However, if it is to avoid merely describing actual states of affairs, such theorizing must make prescriptive claims about how the world ought to be. As a result, behavioral normative democratic theory must scale back its normative claims without thereby abandoning them entirely. Although this may be difficult at times, I can see no other way of constructing a normative democratic theory that is able to address our practical concerns about democratic government without falling into what David Estlund has called a "complacent realism" about politics (Estlund 2008, chap. 14).

[19] There are a number of similarities here to G. A. Cohen's account of fact-sensitive principles of justice. In particular, his distinction between fact-sensitive "principles of regulation" for society and fact-insensitive "fundamental principles" is instructive for our purposes here (G. A. Cohen 2003, 2008).

offer include political autonomy, fairness, the equality of citizens, social stability, substantively correct decisions in politics, and the legitimacy of laws. These are very important moral considerations. Because these goods seem so good, they ought to warrant considerable risk and sacrifice in order to achieve (or maintain) a competent citizenry. If there is even a moderate chance that we could achieve the level of epistemic performance required for these benefits, then we should dedicate both effort and resources to reaching that level. Whether in the form of state-funded educational programs, public spending on research, or individual dedication to self-improvement, we ought to be willing to incur serious costs in order to bring about the goods democracy has to offer.[20]

3.3.2 Focus on Feasibility

The second major advantage of the behavioral approach to democratic theory concerns its focus on feasibility. Much of the time, it is difficult to see how empirical evidence relating to epistemic competence ought to be incorporated into our normative theorizing about democracy. Whereas existing data from psychology and social science is descriptive (i.e., it attempts to describe the current state of our decision-making abilities), democratic theory is normative (e.g., it attempts to determine what sorts of political arrangements ought to be endorsed). As a result, it is often unclear what bearing empirical data has on normative theories of democracy. Now, I argue that normative democratic theory must acknowledge the relevance of this data for its normative theorizing, but it must do so without ceding its ability to criticize actual states of affairs or the ability to expect and demand better.

Normative democratic theory should therefore be wary of two opposing tendencies. On one hand, such theorizing must avoid engaging in free-spinning normative theorizing that denies that any facts about the state of the world are relevant for our understanding of democracy. And on the other hand, normative theorizing, in order to retain its credentials as normative, must avoid merely describing the current state of democratic societies. If normative democratic theory falls into the first trap, it will falsely claim that facts about the world have absolutely no role to play in securing the goods that democracy has to offer. If it succumbs to the second, it will abandon its ability to criticize the status quo.

---

[20] I should here pause to prevent a misunderstanding. In referring to "the goods democracy has to offer" I wish to remain agnostic about whether democracy's benefits are intrinsic or instrumental, procedural or consequentialist. All that I care is that they are goods: they provide us reasons for supporting democratic forms of government. In this way, I do not wish to restrict us to a utilitarian assessment of competence or of democracy more generally.

Ultimately, it is the feasibility or unfeasibility of achieving competence that ought to concern normative democratic theory.[21] Current states of affairs are relevant to normative theorizing only insofar as knowledge of these conditions helps us to determine what we ought to do. In this way, determining whether or not we are currently competent can enable us to make better decisions about the future. If we are already competent, then we should endorse policies and procedures that will maintain our current epistemic abilities. If we are currently incompetent, then we ought to figure out whether achieving competence is a feasible goal, and if so, how best to go about improving our epistemic abilities. In this way, empirical results concerning the current state of our epistemic competence can help us determine the range of feasible possibilities and how to bring about the normatively best alternative.

Normative democratic theory should therefore attempt to balance feasibility constraints against the goods democracy is taken to offer. That is, it ought to weigh the probability of success and the costs associated with initiatives to increase epistemic capacities against the benefits expected to accrue to citizens if they eventually succeed in becoming (or remaining) competent. In this respect behavioral democratic theory has a clear advantage over other approaches to democratic theory: because it employs an empirical model of human decision making, it is better suited to making judgments about the feasibility of attaining various standards of epistemic competence. Whereas other approaches are unable to articulate how current states of affairs are relevant to our assessment of the epistemic demands of various theories of democracy, behavioral democratic theory is able to focus on the feasibility of (and costs associated with) moving from current levels of epistemic performance to the levels required by a given theory of democracy.

3.3.3 Institutional Implications

Behavioral democratic theory must therefore keep in mind both the moral reasons for endorsing democracy and the feasibility of successfully generating the conditions necessary for democracy's proper function. Doing so places a great deal of importance on the proper design of institutions within democracies. If, on a particular theory of democracy, it turns out

---

[21] There is a difficulty here in specifying precisely what is meant by "feasibility." Feasibility must mean something more than just possibility, but it cannot be a strong claim about probable or likely outcomes (e.g., many plans are feasible that are still not probable). For my purposes, it will suffice to understand feasibility as meaning the absence of any compelling contrary considerations. Thus, a political program is feasible if there does not exist any compelling reason to believe that it cannot be brought about. Further explanation of the modal status of feasibility is a difficult task, one that I cannot attempt here.

both that there are significant moral reasons to support democracy and that it is feasible to generate a competent citizenry, then it will be vital to ascertain which institutional mechanisms ought to be employed to ensure that citizens are competent.

The behavioral approach to normative democratic theory thus has the potential to directly affect our practical concerns about democratic government. Because behavioral democratic theory takes as its starting point a realistic assessment of the epistemic capacities of citizens, it can provide practical guidance about what kinds of policies and decisions we ought to endorse. Once we have established the feasibility of attaining a given standard of competence (i.e., the epistemic abilities required by a given theory of democracy), we should be able to determine what kinds of policies and institutions (e.g., public education, enhanced political participation) will help to bring actual abilities in line with that standard. In this way, the primary advantage of a behavioral approach is the ability to use democratic theory as a practical guide for decisions about what kind of policies and arrangements we ought to endorse.

There is a further way in which a behavioral approach to democratic theory can provide us with practical payoffs. This approach allows us to eliminate from our consideration theories of democracy that are unfeasible. If a given theory sets the standard of epistemic competence so high that it simply cannot be met, then behavioral democratic theory will lead us to reject that theory in favor of one that has more reasonable epistemic requirements. This kind of situation, however, is rather unlikely.[22] It is far more likely that we would be led to abandon a theory of democracy not because it was impossible for us to achieve its standard of competence but rather because it would be wrong for us to try.[23] In that case, we

---

[22] Empirical results normally do not reveal the kinds of strict impossibility that would lead us to abandon a theory in this way. It is hard to even imagine what kind of empirical results about the current state of our epistemic abilities would lead us to conclude that it was simply impossible to improve our capacities enough to achieve competence. For an insightful treatment of the role of claims that something is impossible in ethics, see "Impossibility and Morals" (J. Smith 1961) and the work of John Doris (Doris 2002; Stich, Doris, et al. 2010).

[23] Consider the following example: Suppose we support democracy because our favorite normative theory claims that a democracy of competent citizens would lead to the enactment of only just laws. This, I hope we agree, would be a good thing, worthy of great sacrifice and expenditure. But, let's also suppose that our best scientists determine that we all suffer from a cognitive impairment that drops each of us far below the epistemic standard required for democracy to ensure these just results: they reveal that we are all incompetent. Suppose now, that some more of our best scientists come along and demonstrate that the only way to fix this cognitive impairment (and make us all competent) is to perform complicated brain surgery on all adults once they are of voting age. Unfortunately, however, this surgery is very risky: most people die during the operation. It is also horribly painful and very expensive, so few people would willingly undergo the procedure. Assuming that there

ought to settle for a different theory of democracy, one that sets a lower threshold of competence (and, likely but not necessarily, lower expectations for what goods democracy can provide). In this way, a behavioral approach to democratic theory can help us to sort out which political institutions we ought to support by virtue of its ability to winnow down the number of feasible theories of democracy.

A behavioral approach to normative democratic theory can for these reasons serve as a practical guide for our political actions in a way that is ruled out under the three above-mentioned strategies concerning competence. In the case of the factual assertion strategy, we must first establish empirically that our current capacities meet the requirements of a particular theory in order for it to be action-guiding. In the case of the idealizing assumption, we are precluded from using an ideal theory to inform our opinions about actual proposals because we cannot be sure that our assumption about competence actually holds. Following the third strategy, we must be able to generate a justification for treating competence as a moral principle, if we are to use a particular democratic theory as a guide for action. Behavioral democratic theory, on the other hand, allows us to focus on the institutional implications of democratic theory in a way that is unique among the strategies surveyed here. Such an approach encourages us to pursue those institutional arrangements that lend feasibility to our favored theory of democracy, and it allows us to reject institutional proposals from theories that are unfeasible.

---

is an even remotely tolerable alternative (imagine the status quo involved a society where roughly half the laws were just and half moderately unjust), we would be forced to abandon this theory. We need not abandon the theory as an ideal theory; it can still serve that function. But we would have to abandon the theory insofar as we took it to be action-guiding for us. Because it does not describe a situation that we can reasonably hope to bring about, this theory cannot help us to determine what policies and decisions we ought to support.

CHAPTER FOUR

Behavioral Democratic Theory Applied

IN THIS CHAPTER, I narrow my focus once again and present my assessment of the relevance of framing effects for particular normative theories of democracy. Having introduced the phenomenon of framing in chapter 1, I will now show how it ought to affect our thinking about democracy. Drawing on my characterization of the field of democratic theory from chapter 2, I will show the relevance of framing effects for particular categories of normative theories of democracy. I use the description of behavioral democratic theory from chapter 3 to show that emphasizing moral reasons, feasibility constraints, and institutional design leads to important insights about the consequences of framing effects.

My general aims are as follows. First, I hope to show that minimalist theories of democracy—those that place the fewest demands on the political judgment of citizens—can produce only weak moral reasons for endorsing democracy. Second, I claim that in order to be feasible, theories of democracy that incorporate more robust epistemic claims must endorse institutional mechanisms capable of counteracting the pernicious effects of framing. In my last chapter, chapter 5, I discuss some institutional arrangements capable of bolstering political judgment within a democracy.

4.1 PURELY PROCEDURAL THEORIES

From the standpoint of behavioral democratic theory, purely procedural theories of democracy have two important characteristics. First, by virtue of their being purely procedural, they place only the most minimal demands on the judgment of citizens. Second, their pure proceduralism prevents them from making any strong moral claims about the goods democracy has to offer.

It is important to note, however, that many (if not all) theories of democracy that claim to be *purely* procedural cannot, in the end, maintain this claim.[1] The slender moral grounds on which such theories are

---

[1] This point is emphasized and elaborated by David Estlund in chapter 4, "The Limits of Fair Procedure," in *Democratic Authority: A Philosophical Framework* (Estlund 2008).

premised lead many theorists to appropriate nonprocedural reasons for endorsing democracy. In this way, many apparently procedural theories of democracy smuggle in epistemic claims of one sort or another. To the extent that procedural theories incorporate epistemic claims, they manage to bolster their moral case for democracy but only at the expense of exposing them to concerns about the reliability of citizens' judgment.[2]

4.1.1 Social Choice Theory

The normative grounds on which social choice theory recommends democracy (if it is able to recommend democracy at all) are quite limited.[3] Orthodox social choice theory refuses to acknowledge any nonprocedural benefits to democratic decision making; according to this view, it is not the case that we can expect democratic decisions to be wise, good, or just. At best (and this is assuming that Arrow's theorem—the central theoretical result of social choice—does not undermine elections altogether), democratic decision making has procedural value: it sometimes permits individuals to have their preferences reflected in governmental decisions.

Although this is not an insignificant value (all other things equal, we might prefer a system that allows individual preferences to be reflected in decisions to a system that does not), it is not terribly compelling either. In the absence of more substantive values that would recommend democracy, social choice theory can claim only this relationship between preferences and outcomes as moral ground for endorsing democracy.[4] The behavioral approach reveals just how radical a position this is: social choice theory does not recognize any facts about the reliability of voter judgment as at all relevant to an assessment of democracy's value. For such theorists, it wouldn't matter if our political judgment were completely unreliable, because the quality of democratic outcomes do not factor into their account of the value of democratic government.

It should be noted that some political theorists—most obviously Bartels (Bartels 2003a, 2003b) but also Druckman (Druckman 2001b,

---

[2] Adopting Estlund's language (Estlund 2008, 81-82) here, we might say that procedural chastity comes at the expense of strong moral reasons for endorsing democracy. Nonprocedural promiscuity, however, comes with institutional strings attached.

[3] Once again, it should be noted that social choice theory has a complicated normative relationship with democracy (see, e.g., Hardin 1999a, 1999b, 2009). Most of the time, theories of social choice criticize democratic arrangements rather than recommend them. As a result, it is unsurprising that social choice can muster only weak moral reasons for endorsing democracy.

[4] This is not, in and of itself, a criticism of social choice theory. Perhaps such theorists are correct in asserting that there are only weak moral reasons to endorse democratic government. This is certainly at odds, however, with much of the high-flown moral discourse that is currently attached to democracy in contemporary politics.

2004)—have claimed that framing effects might undermine theories of social choice on other grounds. They assert that the prevalence of framing effects in politics could demonstrate the incoherence of the concept of political preferences that is used to ground preference-based theories of democracy.[5] These are complex assertions, and assessing their validity would require entering into a number of technical debates within social choice regarding the nature of preferences.[6] I hope it is clear, however, that if social choice theorists determine that framing effects do not undermine the notion of political preferences, there is nothing for them to worry about regarding the effects of framing on judgment. Once again, the slender procedural grounds on which social choice theory's endorsement of democracy is based insulates it from concerns about the epistemic effects of framing.

4.1.2 Fair Proceduralism

Theories that rely exclusively on procedural fairness can provide only similarly thin grounds for endorsing democracy. Like theories of social choice, fair proceduralism eschews any substantive standards for the evaluation of democratic decisions and claims merely that democracy is a fair procedure for making political decisions in cases where there is widespread disagreement. This may indeed be the case, but taken alone, it is a weak reason for endorsing democracy.

If we take fairness theories at face value, they can offer no nonprocedural reasons for endorsing democracy. For these theories the only reason to endorse democracy is the fact that decisions made democratically give everyone an equal chance of influencing the outcome. On such an account, there can be no substantive constraints on what kinds of decisions will result from democratic procedures: we cannot expect

---

[5] The work of Robert Dahl (1971) and Kenneth Arrow (1950) seems to have set the theoretical paradigm within which most empirical work on democracy is currently carried out. As a result, this research has focused almost exclusively on the relevance of framing effects for preference-based accounts.

[6] Very generally, social choice theorists must decide whether labile political preferences are indeed normatively suspect. This issue is in some ways analogous to recent debates over "adaptive preferences" (Elster 1983; Nussbaum 2000). In both cases a perceived deficiency in the actual preferences of individuals (the contexts of preference formation in the case of adaptive preferences, and the lability of preferences in the case of framing) requires either (1) that we accept preferences as they are and deny that there is any real deficiency, (2) abandon preferences in favor of something else (such as the capabilities approach), or (3) provide a standard for evaluating preferences such that we can identify some as being authoritative and others as deficient. This is a complicated set of issues, however, and I will not expand on them here. For an introduction, see the work of Amartya Sen (1970, 1999a, 1999b) and Cass Sunstein (1984, 1990, 1992, 1993a, 1993b).

democratic decisions to respect standards of truth, prudence, or justice. Once again, the radical nature of this kind of theory needs to be emphasized: such a view manages to avoid making demands on citizens' judgment by claiming procedural fairness alone as the moral ground for democratic government. In this way, such theories are committed to the view that the reliability of our political judgment is of no consequence for democratic theory. This, I hope it will be agreed, is an odd claim, and it results in a conspicuously weak endorsement of democratic government.

David Estlund has criticized fairness theories of democracy for this exclusive reliance on the value of procedural fairness. According to Estlund, such theories are unable to explain why other fair procedures are not deemed appropriate means for making political decisions. He summarizes his argument as follows:

> In brief, the central problem is that procedural fairness, properly conceived, is a very thin and occasional value. Democratic procedures (some of them anyway) might indeed be fair, but this will turn out to be morally too small of a matter to support an account of authority and legitimacy. Procedural fairness alone also cannot explain most of the features of democratic institutions that we are likely to feel are crucial. To anticipate my argument with a one-liner, if what we want is a procedure that is fair to all, why not flip a coin? That is, why not choose a law or policy randomly? (Estlund 2008, 66)

Like elections, a coin toss is a fair procedure. In both cases, everyone has an equal chance of influencing the outcome.[7] In the case of a coin toss, however, it is clear that random decisions could result in flawed, imprudent, and unjust decisions. If this kind of fairness is all that we can expect from democracy, then we have no more reason to support democratic arrangements than we have for subjecting important political decisions to a coin toss. This kind of fairness might be *a* reason to support democracy, but it is too weak a value on which to rest the whole case for democratic government.

Impure Fairness Theories. If fairness theories of democracy are to retain their status as *purely* procedural theories of democracy, they must bite the bullet and accept that the kind of fairness at stake in democracy is, as Estlund puts it, "a very thin and occasional value" (Estlund

---

[7] In a coin toss, our chance of influencing the outcome is zero. In any large election, our chance of influencing the outcome is nearly zero. For consistently pure proceduralists, however, this difference shouldn't matter. As their focus is exclusively on procedures, and not on outcomes, the fact that both procedures treat everyone equally should be all that matters. This issue and many others are treated at length in chapter 4, "The Limits of Fair Procedure," in Estlund (2008).

2008, 66). Rather than accept this view, however, many fairness theories of democracy instead covertly conjoin to their account a number of substantive claims about the reliability of democratic decision making.[8] The resulting impure fairness theories provide us with stronger moral reasons for endorsing democracy, but they do so at the expense of their claims about procedural purity.[9] Further, to the extent that they embrace nonprocedural values, these theories must rely on the political judgment of citizens in order to bring about the substantive results that democracy is now held to offer and thus must contend with the implications of the behavioral model of choice I have been developing.

To see how framing effects threaten these impure fairness theories, consider the following possibility. One of the most common ways in which fairness theories smuggle in epistemic claims concerns long-term prospects for ensuring the fairness of democratic procedures.[10] Many such theories require citizens to exercise good judgment to refrain from enacting measures that would erode the procedural fairness of democratic elections. For instance, the judgment of citizens must be relied on not to pass laws disenfranchising large portions of the population or installing an absolute sovereign.

Now, Kahneman and Tversky's positive account of framing effects, called prospect theory (Kahneman and Tversky 2000a, 2000d), predicts that when faced with potential gains, individuals can be expected to exhibit risk-averse behavior, but when presented with potential losses they will be risk-seeking (Thaler, Tversky, et al. 1997). Prospect theory has thus been taken to entail loss aversion: humans are more responsive to frames that emphasize potential losses than they are to frames that emphasize potential gains (Ariely et al. 2005; Camerer 2005; Novemsky and Kahneman 2005a, 2005b).[11]

---

[8] Estlund criticizes Jeremy Waldron (Waldron 1999c) in particular (Estlund 2000, 2008), but other theorists (e.g., Robert Dahl) also seem to move illicitly from procedural to epistemic reasons for endorsing democracy. Although I cannot substantiate these claims here, if such theorists are at all concerned about the reliability of individual political judgment in a democracy, then they are not entitled to their claims about pure proceduralism. Purely procedural theories are radical in a way that is quite incongruous with the more conventional approach to democratic institutions that theorists like Waldron and Dahl otherwise present.

[9] In contrast with modified procedural theories (section 4.3), these theories do not acknowledge their commitment to nonprocedural values: they claim to be purely procedural, but on closer inspection, they cannot sustain this purity. As a result, I will treat them separately from modified procedural theories. It should be noted, however, that modified procedural theories will also have to contend with the worries about framing effects outlined below.

[10] For evidence that Waldron relies on this kind of claim, see Waldron (1999c, 221–231).

[11] Loss aversion has been shown to have implications for issues as diverse as stock market behavior (Bernartzi and Thaler 1995), organ transplantation (Johnson and Goldstein

Prospect theory's predictions about loss aversion can be interpreted as a threat to impure fairness theories that rely on the judgment of voters to preserve the long-term fairness of democratic procedures. In particular, it is possible that our aversion to loss could be seized on to justify encroachment on the fairness of democracy. This could take any number of forms, but most provocatively, it could be manifested in attempts to disenfranchise individuals or groups who pose a perceived risk to the interests of the democratic majority. The empirical literature indicates that it might be possible to manipulate frames for political issues in such a way as to ensure that citizens are inclined to trade long-term political fairness for short-term security. If this were the case, then our susceptibility to framing effects would pose a direct threat to the fairness of democracy: over time, citizens could be led to make decisions that erode procedural fairness.

It is important to note, however, that prospect theory indicates only that we will be more responsive to frames that emphasize losses; it says nothing about the content of those frames.[12] Our susceptibility to framing is in this way formal: we are averse to losses, but there is usually the possibility of reframing particular decision problems in terms of losses or in terms of gains.[13] As long as it remains possible to frame the loss of fairness as a loss, then all is not lost. Impure fairness theories, however, ought to be particularly wary of any political climate in which perceived risks (e.g., from saboteurs, communists, or terrorists) are framed in terms of losses, while attempts to protect fairness are captured in less effective gain frames. For this reason, impure fairness theories need to acknowledge their reliance on the judgment of citizens and pursue institutional arrangements that can secure the quality of those judgments. Institutions can be designed in such a way as to prevent our aversion to loss from being exploited, but in order to justify these institutions it is imperative that we acknowledge the role of individual political judgment in securing the fairness of democratic procedures.[14]

2003), environmental regulation (Sunstein 2005b), war (Nincic 1997; Levy 2000), and reactions to terrorism (Sunstein 2003).

[12] Although some interesting research has been conducted on how people make trade-offs between civil liberties and risks from terrorism (Viscusi and Zeckhauser 2003), as well as on how different media frames for terrorism affect potential voters (Schnell and Callaghan 2005), there is currently no evidence that our susceptibility to framing effects will always lead us to neglect fairness. Related research on the effects of framing—including the endowment effect (Kahneman, Knetsch, et al. 2000b) and the status quo bias (Baron 1995)—might be interpreted to imply the opposite: that individual decision makers will be extremely unlikely to give up procedural constraints on fairness. This is especially true if individuals view civil liberties as an important part of their initial set of political entitlements.

[13] This is what motivates concerns about the use of default rules and starting points (see especially Sunstein and Thaler 2008 here).

[14] In chapter 5 (especially section 5.1), I explore various institutional mechanisms that can prevent particular perspectives from gaining a monopoly over the framing of political

Advocates of fair proceduralism face a choice: they can either own up to how thin a purely procedural account of fairness really is, or they can abandon pure proceduralism in favor of a theory of democracy that incorporates claims about the epistemic reliability of democratic decision making. If they do the former, then we should note that the moral grounds on which they recommend democracy are very weak. If they pursue the latter course, they must contend with empirical challenges to their claims about the reliability of democratic decision making and endorse institutional arrangements that respond to these challenges.

4.1.3 Deep Deliberative Democracy

Because theories of deep deliberative democracy also reject procedure-independent standards for evaluating democratic outcomes, their focus must also be on the value of democratic procedures themselves. Deep deliberative theories claim that democratic procedures are legitimate solely by virtue of their procedural value (e.g., being public, treating persons equally, and being accessible).[15] Such theories thus cannot expect democratic decisions to be good, prudent, or just. As a result, these procedural values—despite being more compelling than mere procedural fairness—still provide us with very limited grounds on which to endorse democracy. By virtue of being purely procedural, deep deliberative theories must avoid making any substantive claims about how democracies will decide important issues: unless we build in claims about the tendency of democratic decisions to be correct (when evaluated against procedure-independent standards), we are not entitled to any substantive claims about how democracies will decide questions about rights, justice, or anything else.

Once again, this is a counterintuitive claim. Most of us tend to associate the value of democratic government, at least to some extent, with the kind of decisions that issue from such systems.[16] But according to the

---

decisions. These institutional mechanisms will be of central importance to the epistemic claims of impure fairness theories.

[15] There are a number of important controversies, complications, and qualifications regarding these procedural values. For instance, it remains necessary to specify the domain over which they are to be applied (e.g., whether any decision making can be done in secret, whether adults ought to be treated differently from minors, and whether political processes may exclude noncitizens). These details cannot, however, be treated here. For an analysis of these and related concerns, see the work of Hugh Baxter (2011).

[16] I don't mean to claim that because such views are counterintuitive, that they must be incorrect. Instead, I simply want to point out that purely procedural theories are in fact quite radical. They claim, contrary to much contemporary discourse about democracy, that the moral case for democracy relies exclusively on procedural values. This results in a significantly weaker endorsement of democracy than might be expected.

deep deliberativist, this is a mistake. Democratic procedures alone recommend democracy on this view.

As in the case of fairness theories, however, there is a temptation here to overstep the bounds of pure proceduralism.[17] To see why this is the case, consider the following. According to a deep theory of deliberative democracy, even if procedural values are initially satisfied (e.g., democratic procedures are at some moment in time public, equal, and accessible), there is no guarantee that these procedural values will endure. Unless we incorporate epistemic claims about the reliability of democratic decisions, there is no compelling reason to think that over time, democracies will continue to respect such values. Given that purely procedural theories refuse to make any claims about the quality of democratic outcomes, they cannot rely on the good judgment of citizens to respect cherished procedural values.[18] Public, equal, and accessible decision making could, on this view, lead to decisions that empower a secretive, unequal, and exclusive government.

Impure Deliberative Theories.   As a result, deep deliberative theories can either accept the possibility that deliberative democracy might be self-defeating, or they can choose to rely on the judgment of citizens to maintain the procedural value of democracy. If deep deliberativists opt to remain purely procedural, they must acknowledge that their view admits the possibility that democratic decisions might generate nondemocratic outcomes. If they opt to abandon procedural purity and make claims about the reliability of democratic decision making, they ought to be concerned with empirical results that demonstrate how our susceptibility to framing effects could undermine these procedural standards.

As in the case of fairness theories, the empirical literature on framing effects will be of concern to impure deliberative theories primarily insofar as this literature indicates that our decision making might be particularly susceptible to framing in domains where procedural values are at

[17] The work of Jürgen Habermas appears to move illicitly between a pure and impure proceduralism (Habermas 1996; Habermas et al. 1998). However, Habermas's more recent work seems to wholeheartedly embrace an epistemic version of deliberative democracy (Habermas 2005, 2006). As a result, I am unsure how to properly characterize his position. See his essay "Political Communication in Media Society: Does Democracy Still Enjoy an Epistemic Dimension? The Impact of Normative Theory on Empirical Research" (Habermas 2006).

[18] It might be possible, if we greatly circumscribe the domain over which democratic decision making is allowed to range, to protect some procedural values by means of constitutional entrenchment and other countermajoritarian procedures. Even so, however, we must rely on the good judgment of citizens and legislators to respect the bounds set by a constitution or other laws. Unless we rely on the good judgment of citizens, at least to some extent, we simply cannot expect much from democracy.

issue. For instance, if framing effects predictably lead to choices that favor inequality, then deliberative democrats would have cause for worry about the possibility of ensuring the long-term equality of democratic government. Although it is clear that framing does affect decision making about such matters,[19] the direction in which the decisions are biased (i.e., toward equality or inequality) depends on specific conditions (Kahneman, Knetsch, et al. 2000a, 2000b). Some frames lead individuals to make choices that promote equality, while other frames incline people toward choices that reduce it. Once again, impure deliberative theories must therefore consider how research on framing effects (and prospect theory in particular) can be used to generate institutional mechanisms capable of ensuring that democratic decisions will not be biased against procedural values.

4.2 STABILITY THEORIES

Stability theories of democracy emphasize the importance of one expected product of democratic government: social stability. This stability, it is argued, is due to the ability of elections to serve as an agreeable means for powerful groups to share political control. Thus, rather than resort to open violence and bloodshed, political elites will agree to abide by the results of regular elections by citizens. This arrangement is expected to be congenial to both those who would compete to be rulers and those who would be ruled. The behavioral approach to democratic theory shows that there are empirical reasons to be suspicious of even the limited moral grounds such theories propose in favor of democratic government.

4.2.1 Austere Stability Theories

Austere stability theories, with their reluctance to propose mechanisms that would improve the quality of decision making by democratic governments, rely on the maintenance of social stability for the whole of their moral case for democratic government. On this view, we should not expect the rule of democratically elected leaders to conduce to the greater good of citizens, except insofar as the avoidance of violent conflict turns out to be in their interests.

Interestingly, the austere stability theorist's descriptive claims about the stabilizing effects of democracy are actually strengthened by evidence of framing. Research appears to show that the choice set within which

---

[19] Research has documented framing effects in questions concerning both justice (Kinsey et al. 1991; Roberts et al. 1994; Gamliel and Peer 2006) and equality (Brewer 2002, 2007; Brewer and Gross 2005).

options are embedded can often influence individuals' choices. Cass Sunstein explains this effect of framing in terms of what he calls "extremeness aversion":

> People are averse to extremes. Whether an option is extreme depends on the stated alternatives. Extremeness aversion gives rise to compromise effects. As between given alternatives, people seek a compromise. In this as in other respects, the framing of choice matters; the introduction of (unchosen, apparently irrelevant) alternatives into the frame can alter the outcome. When, for example, people are choosing between some small radio A and a mid-size radio B, most may well choose A; but the introduction of a third, large radio C is likely to lead many people to choose B instead. Thus the introduction of a third, unchosen (and in that sense irrelevant) option may produce a switch in choice as between two options. Almost everyone has had an experience of switching to (say) the second most expensive item on some menu of options, and of doing so partly because of the presence of the very most expensive item. (Sunstein 1997, 1181–1182).

This kind of context dependence is not restricted to the avoidance of extremes: various trade-off, compromise, and polarization effects can occur as a result of the context in which options are presented (Simonson and Tversky 1992; Tversky and Simonson 2000).[20] Because choices are in this way sensitive to the contexts in which they are elicited (Slovic 2000; Lichtenstein and Slovic 2006), control over the statement of options entails some amount of control over the eventual choices:[21] by manipulating the options presented, it might be possible to control the content of individual preferences.

If political elites have control over the framing of political options in democratic elections, then (if they exercise that control wisely) they can be expected to restrict some individuals' political preferences to the set they present. It should be noted that these would be, under the standard understanding of political preferences, the *real* preferences of citizens. As a result, those citizens whose choices were constructed with the help of

---

[20] One interesting account of the logical structure of framing effects (Gold and List 2004) claims that our susceptibility to frames should be understood as the result of a sequential process of decision making in which a target proposition is considered against a set of background options. According to Gold and List, framing effects occur when differences in the order in which background options are considered result in different decisions. If this account is correct, then framing effects are due to the context-dependence of our preferences. In particular, framing effects result from the fact that our preferences may vary depending on the set of options under consideration at a given time (List 2004).

[21] Context-dependence has been observed in legal decision making as well. The set of options presented to a jury has predictable effects on eventual choices (Kelman et al. 1996).

political elites could be expected to be genuinely satisfied if their favored elites come to power.

In this way, framing effects bolster the austere minimalist's assertion that individuals will judge it to be in their best interest to pursue the stability provided by elections, even if it were sometimes the case that their real interests might be served better by violent revolution. Given the control exercised over their preferences by elites, a citizen's decision to support a particular political leader may seem normatively deficient, but it will likely not appear so to the citizens themselves (at least not in the short term).[22] In fact, in such a situation the formation of an individual's political preferences may appear to be entirely autonomous. Thus, framing effects might provide some empirical support for the descriptive claim that democratic elections (where the preferences of voters have been shaped, in part, by the elites vying for power) will provide some measure of social stability.

If this is the case, however, framing effects may undermine the stability theorist's moral case for democracy. In the situation described above, individuals satisfy preferences that do not conduce to their own well-being. In such cases social stability comes at the cost of individual welfare, instead of promoting it. If this is the case, then the stability that initially recommends such theories proves to be stability for the wrong reasons: here citizens abide by the decisions of elites largely as a result of a process of manipulation. It is hard to see how this kind of stability (recall that, according to the austere minimalist, this is the only good that recommends democracy) ought to count as a reason to endorse democracy. For this reason, the kind of stability that austere stability theories rely on appears to provide a very weak moral basis for democratic government.

4.2.2 Augmented Stability Theories

In chapter 2 (section 2.2.2), I introduced three proposals for improving the quality of democratic decision making (over that of austere theories): competition, selection, and political freedom. In each case, a theory of democratic government emphasizing stability is modified to include an account of how various mechanisms can be expected to lead to good political decisions (where political decisions are measured against an independent standard). In each case the mechanisms at issue require that at least some individuals (e.g., political leaders) exercise sound political judgment.

In the case of competition, good judgment on the part of political leaders must be exercised in order to discern and promote the desires of

---

[22] For conditions under which well-being might diverge from preference-satisfaction, see the articles anthologized in Olsaretti (2006).

voters; and voters themselves must be relied on to exercise good judgment in selecting leaders that have the requisite powers of discernment.[23] It is only in this way that competition between political elites—carried out by responding to voter preferences—can successfully lead to good political outcomes (as misdiagnosing preferences or designing policies that are nonresponsive will not lead to the desired outcomes). In the case of selection, the proposed augmentation claims that competition will lead to the selection of a class of politically competent leaders. In order for this to be the case, there must exist a pool of individuals who have good political judgment, from which the competitive process can select. In the political freedom case, it is asserted that, in order to endure, democratic arrangements must protect fundamental political rights (e.g., freedom of speech and political participation). In these instances, political leaders must possess powers of political judgment that reliably ensure the protection of these freedoms.[24]

In this way, augmented stability theories require that at least some individuals possess reliable epistemic capacities in order to ensure that democratic outcomes are better than could be expected by the austere stability theorist. If no one were politically competent, then the proposed augmentations would fail, and such theories would have nothing to offer other than the avoidance of violent struggles for political power. As a result, the empirical literature on framing effects will be relevant to such theories primarily insofar as it indicates whether or not political leaders can actually be expected to have more reliable epistemic abilities than average citizens.[25]

There are general empirical reasons (unrelated to framing effects) for being suspicious of the reliability of the judgment of many of the individuals whom we currently call political experts (Tetlock 2005; Menand 2005). Recently, there has also been a substantial amount of research into whether expertise, usually determined by education and experience, helps us to avoid framing effects. This research is part of a broader attempt to determine whether various personal characteristics (e.g., gender[26] or

---

[23] Additionally, in order for the satisfaction of voter preferences to lead to substantively good political decisions being made, it must be the case that individual preferences satisfy certain conditions of rationality (i.e., it must be the case that their preferences are not self-destructive or incoherent).

[24] This is not an insignificant demand, as it may sometimes be the case that the repeal of such political freedoms would be in the short-term interest of elites. In these cases, political leaders must be capable of realizing that it is in the long-term interest of democracy to preserve these political freedoms.

[25] My comments in the following section draw on a helpful survey of the empirical literature provided by Shafir and LeBoeuf (2002).

[26] Results here have been mixed, with no consensus as to whether gender differences are at all significant (Stoddard and Fern 1999; Blais and Weber 2001; Bateman et al. 2002;

age[27]) correlate with susceptibility to framing. A number of prominent studies have indicated that neither education nor professional experience is sufficient to insulate decision making from the effects of framing. These results have been particularly striking in medical contexts, where physicians have repeatedly demonstrated a susceptibility to frames roughly equivalent to that of patients (McNeil et al. 1982; Redelmeier and Tversky 1990; Redelmeier and Shafir 1995). The empirical evidence is not conclusive for all domains,[28] but there are clearly many instances where expertise does not render individuals immune to framing effects.[29] As a result, it seems unwise to put too much weight on the reliability of experts in instances where we are concerned about the efficacy of framing.

Augmented stability theories, with their heavy reliance on the judgment of experts, thus ought to be concerned about epistemic deficiencies stemming from our susceptibility to framing. In order to generate stronger reasons for endorsing democracy than their austere counterpart, such theories must trust the judgment of political elites. However, if such theories doubt the reliability of citizens in general, there seems to be little empirical reason to think that the judgment of elites will be any better. Augmented stability theories thus seem unable to propose more compelling reasons to support democracy than their austere counterparts.

4.3 Modified Procedural Theories

Modified procedural theories recognize two kinds of value in democratic government: procedural and epistemic. Such theories regard democracy as both intrinsically and instrumentally valuable. In general, they claim

---

Joslyn and Haider-Markel 2002; Levin, Gaeth, et al. 2002; Hasseldine and Hite 2003; A. Simon, Fagley, et al. 2004; Hiscox 2006).

[27] There is little empirical agreement on this issue, as studies yield contradictory results (Takemura 1994; Camerer 1995; Sieck and Yates 1997; Mayhorn et al. 2002; Kim et al. 2005; Ronnlund et al. 2005).

[28] Results from other fields are less robust but also support the view that expertise is not a reliable indicator of insusceptibility to framing effects (Neale and Northcraft 1986; Duchon et al. 1989; Loke and Lau 1992; Loke and Tan 1992; Fatas et al. 2007).

[29] A different criterion has also been used to monitor susceptibility to framing: the so-called need for cognition (NC) variable (Cacioppo and Petty 1982) reflects the extent (usually self-reported) to which individuals enjoy puzzle-solving and other reasoning tasks. Studies here too are inconclusive, with researchers generating mixed results (S. Smith and Levin 1996; Levin, Gaeth, et al. 2002; LeBoeuf and Shafir 2003). In some studies, James Druckman (2004) and others (Druckman and Nelson 2003) have combined NC scores with other indicators of political expertise (e.g., education and experience) to show that that cognitively-inclined individuals with high degrees of expertise are less susceptible to framing effects but that they also tend to exhibit overconfidence in their judgments.

that democratic processes ensure the legitimacy of government, and that democratic decisions ensure good political outcomes. As a result of their recognition of these two kinds of value, modified procedural theorists must rely on the political judgment of citizens to perform two distinct functions: to preserve the procedural value of democracy and to make correct decisions regarding political issues. These theories are thus heavily invested in epistemic reliability of citizens' judgment. As a consequence, modified procedural theories must be wary of the potentially negative effects that framing could have on either the procedural legitimacy of democratic processes or on the epistemic value of democratic decisions.

I have already dealt with the threat that framing effects pose to procedural values (see my treatment of impure theories in sections 4.1.2 and 4.1.3), and so I will focus here on the challenge that framing effects pose to the epistemic value of democratic government. It should not be forgotten, however, that the epistemic concerns of modified theories are not exhausted by those raised below.

4.3.1 Unorthodox Social Choice Theory

Social choice theory, in its orthodox formulations, emphasizes the procedural value of ensuring that governmental policies are responsive to individual preferences. Theories of social choice, however, have been disparaged for the kinds of preferences they ascribe to citizens. In particular, they have been criticized for the narrow self-interest that citizens are expected to display at the ballot box. The unorthodox variant of social choice that I consider here differs in that it expects citizens to use their votes to help bring about political outcomes that they judge to be in the public interest.[30] In order to generate these outcomes, however, institutions must be designed in order to effectively mobilize citizens' moral judgments. Many of the institutional arrangements required to extract epistemic value from voters are quite familiar and uncontroversial.[31] Other proposed institutional reforms, however, are rather novel.

Perhaps the most radical proposal of this kind involves the conditions of anonymity currently surrounding most democratic elections. In "Unveiling the Vote" Brennan and Pettit (1990) argue for relaxing the anonymity condition that currently applies to most voting procedures in

---

[30] This variant is developed by Geoffrey Brennan and others in numerous publications (Brennan and Lomasky 1989, 1993; Brennan and Hamlin 2000, 2002; Brennan and Pettit 2002, 2004).

[31] For instance, Brennan and Hamlin (2000) discuss some rather innocuous electoral reforms, representation schemes, political party systems, and recommendations for the separation of powers.

democratic countries; they call for requiring the limited publicity of one's vote. By calling individuals to account for the direction of their votes, they hope to provide citizens with an added incentive to vote in morally responsible ways. Thus, they wish to induce more citizens to use their votes to bring about the common good, rather than to use them in an attempt to secure their own private interests.

This is, as the authors readily admit, a controversial proposal. It is controversial for a number of reasons, but most important for our purposes, it seeks to secure an epistemic good (i.e., generating good political outcomes) at the expense of a procedural value of democratic government. The secrecy of one's ballot is, on most accounts, valuable because it ensures the procedural fairness of elections. Unveiling the vote would be a greater inconvenience to some (e.g., those dissenters whose construal of the common good diverges from the judgment of their neighbors) than to others (e.g., those who share the views of their community). There is a sense, therefore, in which a public vote would represent a diminution in the fairness of democratic procedures.[32] It is asserted, however, that this diminution in fairness is worth it because of the increased epistemic value of democratic elections that would result.

This purported epistemic value, it should be noted, requires that individual citizens possess reliable political judgment. The considered moral judgment of citizens about what is in the common interest must actually be a good guide to the public interest in order for this trade-off of procedural for epistemic value to be worthwhile. To paraphrase the authors, this trade-off only makes sense "to the extent that voters can be relied on to make their judgments of the common good tolerably accurately" (Brennan and Pettit 1990, 316).

The epistemic value of these decisions, however, is directly threatened by our susceptibility to framing. Unless we can ensure that our political judgments are not swayed by irrelevant considerations stemming from the framing of our choices, we have no assurance that our judgments will in fact be tolerably accurate. Empirical research on framing effects is thus relevant to unorthodox social choice insofar as this research can help to bear out the epistemic claims of this theory. If we cannot actually expect our political judgments to be correct (when evaluated in terms of independent standards like truth or justice), then there is nothing more to recommend democracy on this theory than the bare procedural grounds proposed by orthodox versions of social choice.

---

[32] I should note that, in order to accommodate this view, we require a different understanding of fairness than was presented in section 4.1.2. There, fairness was taken to require equal chances for influencing democratic outcomes. The kind of fairness at issue here concerns the distribution of burdens in a democracy.

4.3.2 Epistemic Deliberative Democracy

Epistemic theories of deliberative democracy will similarly find framing effects to be most important insofar as they represent a challenge to proposals that would attempt to capitalize on the epistemic potential of democracy. In cases where there is a procedural cost to the reform of institutions, the epistemic value of these reforms might be challenged on grounds that the susceptibility of human judgment to framing effects nullifies any proposed epistemic gains. In such cases, the epistemic deliberativist will be required to argue for the feasibility of attaining the requisite reliability of political judgment. The most obvious way to argue for this feasibility would be to propose institutional mechanisms for the improvement of our judgment.

One thing that is interesting about epistemic theories of deliberative democracy is the extent to which epistemic considerations already seem to have carried the day. The procedural ideals of deliberation are reflected only sparingly in the actual procedures of most democratic governments. Instead, concessions to the exigencies of political circumstance have guided the design of most democratic institutions: majority rule can thus be seen as a degraded version of consensus; political representation as an oftentimes inadequate substitute for direct democracy; time limits on debate as perversions of the ideal of unconstrained deliberation; and mechanisms permitting bargaining as cynical attempts to ensure workable political outcomes. If this is indeed the case, and electoral arrangements are most often designed with substantive, rather than procedural goals in mind, then the epistemic deliberativist is already very committed to the epistemic value of democratic decision making.

To the extent that deliberativists are thus committed, they should be expected to provide arguments explaining why the epistemic value of democracy survives challenges on the basis of framing effects and other cognitive pathologies. The behavioral model of human decision making predicts that our judgments will be responsive to the framing of our choices. As a result, we cannot merely assume that the proper conditions for reliable political judgment will be in place: our judgment is not infallible, and if we must rely on this judgment, we cannot afford to be complacent about the conditions required for sound decision making. If epistemic theories of deliberative democracy are to be entitled to claims about the reliability of democratic decision making, they must be willing to propose mechanisms capable of ensuring that democratic decision making does not go awry.

As a result, epistemic theories of deliberative democracy ought to endorse institutions capable of reducing the pernicious effects of framing. Insofar as framing effects are capable of leading individuals to make substantively incorrect judgments, then any theory that relies on democracy's truth- or justice-seeking potential as a reason for endorsing democratic government ought to be willing to dedicate resources to the improvement of democratic decision making. Our susceptibility to framing counts as an important threat to the correctness of democratic decisions and thus merits serious attention by epistemic deliberative theories.

4.3.3 Epistemic Proceduralism

Epistemic proceduralism, by virtue of the central role played by epistemic considerations within the theory, must contend with a number of distinct empirical challenges regarding the competence of citizens. Because epistemic proceduralism construes the legitimacy of democratic government as contingent on its ability to track the truth (at least to some extent) about politics, it cannot rely on the procedural value of democracy unless this epistemic value is assured. Framing effects will therefore be relevant to epistemic proceduralism in at least three ways. First, empirical research could be mustered to challenge the assertion that democratic decision making is better than random.[33] Second, data on framing effects will be relevant to the choice of political procedures from among those that meet with general acceptability.[34] Third, in a way similar to other modified procedural theories, institutional recommendations that would increase the epistemic value of democracy at the cost of procedural values can be criticized empirically for doing so in ways that fail to generate a net democratic benefit.

First, it should be noted there is currently not enough data to quantify the extent to which framing effects undermine our political judgment. As a result, we cannot come to any satisfactory assessment about whether framing effects cause our political judgment to be worse than random. It is simply too early on in this research to make such a conclusion. Given that the extent of our susceptibility to political framing effects cannot yet be specified, the first challenge appears inconclusive.

The second way in which framing effects will be relevant for epistemic proceduralism involves the choice among political systems that meet the general acceptability requirement on political justification. Epistemic proceduralism endorses that system of political decision making that is epistemically best, from among the set of systems that meets with general

---

[33] Estlund (2008) discusses a version of this challenge in chapter 9, "How Would Democracy Know?".

[34] For Estlund's (2008) claim that democracy is the epistemically best system that meets with general acceptability, see chapter 6, "Epistemic Proceduralism."

acceptability. For our purposes here it will suffice to consider two competing institutional arrangements: majority rule and lottery voting.[35]

Under a system of lottery voting, citizens register their opinion on
some political issue (e.g., the election of a representative or the enactment
of a piece of legislation) by means of a ballot.[36] Subsequently, all ballots
are gathered together, and one is selected at random. The selected ballot
carries the day, and the political issue is decided solely in accordance with
that ballot. In this way, each citizen has an equal chance of being decisive. Lottery voting thus differs from systems of majority-rule in that it
is nonaggregative: it does not count votes, it simply picks a winner from
among the ballots cast.

Lottery voting is in some ways quite similar to more familiar electoral arrangements.[37] Indeed, in many instances, the two systems can be
expected to yield similar political results—at least in the long run. However, it appears to be an open question whether lottery voting or majority
rule has more epistemic value (i.e., which does a better job of making
correct political judgments) and under what kind of conditions.

It therefore seems to be an interesting empirical question whether lottery voting might, in certain circumstances, have an epistemic advantage
over majority rule. For instance, if our susceptibility to framing effects
leaves us prone to informational cascades[38] or to the status quo bias,
then aggregative procedures may not be the best means of extracting correct answers from large populations. Instead, a lottery system may yield
greater epistemic value.[39] Epistemic proceduralism could use empirical
research into the extent and influence of framing to determine which system of voting is capable of extracting the greatest epistemic value from
citizens' judgments.

[35] I assume, but will not argue, that both systems meet the general acceptability requirement. Estlund seems to indicate that Queen for a Day, his own version of lottery voting, is
generally acceptable (Estlund 1997a, 191–194).

[36] The standard treatment of lottery voting is found in the work of Akhil Amar (1984,
1995), but there are numerous other formulations as well (Elster 1988; Wolff 1998; Duxbury 1999; Goodwin 2005; Saunders 2010).

[37] A sufficiently broad understanding of democratic procedures will recognize systems
like lottery voting as species of democracy. Estlund himself endorses a very expansive definition, claiming, "What I will mean by 'democracy' is the collective authorization of laws and
policies by the people subject to them" (Estlund 2008, 38). As a result, he can claim that
both majority rule and lottery voting procedures are democratic (Estlund 1997a, 192–193).
My interest here is not whether lottery voting is democratic but whether or not it should be
recommended by the epistemic proceduralist. As a result, my comments here are intended
as friendly additions to the theory.

[38] For these pathologies and their potential relevance for democratic decision making, see
the work of Cass Sunstein (Kuran and Sunstein 1999; Sunstein 2001, 2005a, 2006, 2009a).

[39] Admittedly, this is merely conjecture. I know of no empirical evidence to support this
claim.

The third respect in which framing effects will be relevant to epistemic proceduralism involves the design of democratic institutions. In many instances, improving the epistemic value of group decision making requires making trade-offs against procedural constraints on democratic processes.[40] When this is the case, the proposed epistemic gains ought to be evaluated in light of relevant empirical data, including data on framing effects. Proposals to generate epistemic gains at the cost of procedural values ought to consider whether our susceptibility to framing effects makes it less likely that those epistemic gains will actually be forthcoming. In particular, initiatives that would reform institutions of political deliberation so as to make them more epistemically fruitful should be viewed with some empirical skepticism.[41] In these cases, we should consider whether our susceptibility to framing would hinder the success of epistemically oriented institutions.

4.4 Epistemic Theories

The last category of democratic theories to consider comprises epistemic theories of democracy. These theories, by virtue of the fact that they place the weightiest epistemic demands on the judgment of citizens, are also most dependent on empirical premises about competence. In order to be feasible, these theories must be very concerned about the epistemic capacities of citizens and should muster every effort to ensure that citizens have the powers of judgment they require. In what follows, I will point out some of the more controversial empirical claims on which these theories rely and attempt to demonstrate where empirical research will be most relevant for assessing the feasibility of such theories.

4.4.1 Dialogical Democracy

Talisse's epistemological justification of democracy, by virtue of its explicit focus on the conditions under which individuals can express their epistemic agency, requires that citizens cultivate a whole range

[40] For a particularly vivid example of this sort, see David Estlund's proposal regarding progressive vouchers in "Political Quality" (2002b). Here Estlund presents an epistemic argument against a certain kind of political egalitarianism (i.e., the equality of political influence). In this way, he advocates loosening procedural constraints on equality in order to improve the quality of political decisions.

[41] I am thinking, for example, of David Estlund's proposal for deploying countervailing deviations to compensate for epistemically destructive influences on political deliberation. See chapter 10, "The Real Speech Situation" (Estlund 2008) and previous works (Estlund 2001a, 2001b, 2005).

of epistemic capabilities. Although he does not directly address framing effects, Talisse is cognizant of the difficulties presented by various cognitive biases to his theory, and he focuses his attention on assorted social pathologies that may lead us to hold false beliefs. Talisse thus presents a number of institutional mechanisms capable of addressing problems of ignorance, apathy, and discourse failure. These include informational, educational, and electoral proposals for improving public discourse (Talisse 2009a, chap. 5). Similarly, framing effects are a problem for dialogical democracy insofar as they are capable of preventing us from becoming proper epistemic agents. That is, if framing effects can lead us to be swayed by bad evidence or to be unreasonably resistant to good reasons, Talisse must worry about the possibility that framing could prevent the conditions that justify democracy from ever coming to be.[42]

On Talisse's account, a properly functioning democracy seems to involve at least two elements: the first is a forum for public deliberation; the second is a mechanism enabling citizens to make collective decisions.[43] The most pressing epistemic challenge to Talisse's account, I believe, stems from the possibility that these two elements might come into conflict with one another. In particular, dialogical democrats must be concerned that democratic decisions might undermine the conditions of openness and exchange so important to the dialogical defense of democracy, and they must also worry that protecting such conditions might require that we take so many political questions off the table that we prevent a polity from ruling itself.

Given the possibility that a dialogical democracy could be self-undermining in these ways, it would be extremely helpful to know whether our susceptibility to framing effects makes it likely that citizens will undermine epistemic agency by either: (1) making collective decisions that threaten the conditions of public deliberation (e.g., by limiting political speech), or (2) unduly constricting the domain of democratic decision making (e.g., by abdicating democratic control of important decisions). Although I don't know of any research at present that bears directly on

[42] Talisse associates these conditions with a "politics of engagement" (Talisse 2009a, 150–155).

[43] To see how these two elements may diverge, imagine first a constitutional monarchy that provides ideal conditions for the exchange of reasons and the cultivation of true beliefs, but where many important decisions are not made democratically (instead, they are made by the monarch). Next, imagine a direct democracy where political speech has been repressed by popular decree. Talisse argues that neither arrangement is capable of cultivating proper epistemic agency (the first because it does not allow the polity to make its own decisions, the second because it does not provide a proper forum for public deliberation).

these issues, I am hopeful that future studies of political framing effects will be capable of elucidating just how feasible Talisse's epistemically perfectionist state really is.[44]

4.4.2 Condorcetian Theories

There are at least two ways in which the empirical literature on framing effects bears on Condorcetian theories of democracy. First, susceptibility to framing might be interpreted as a direct challenge to the requirement that individuals possess the epistemic abilities required by Condorcet's jury theorem. That is, we could view framing as evidence that individuals do not, on average, have a better than random chance of getting the correct answer to political questions. If this were the case, then the jury theorem would not provide any reason to support democratic forms of government.

Second, framing effects might be seen to undermine Condorcetian theories of democracy because of what they reveal about the independence of voters.[45] On this interpretation, the problem with framing effects is not what they reveal about competence but rather concerns the condition—required by the jury theorem—that individual votes be statistically independent of one another. In this way, research on framing could be relevant to understanding the relationship that obtains between the votes of individual citizens. Specifically, framing effects could prevent voters who are swayed by frames from contributing to the epistemic reliability of the group. On this view, individuals who successfully frame political debates could be construed as particularly influential opinion leaders (Estlund 1994). If these framers were few in number and had enough influence over other voters, then it might be the case that the effective size of the electorate (those who are providing independent epistemic input) could be so small that the aggregation of their votes would not yield the sharp statistical upswing toward certainty that is usually characteristic of Condorcet's jury theorem.[46]

---

[44] In this regard, proposals for insulating political outcomes from flawed democratic decision making will be particularly relevant (see section 5.2 below).

[45] The jury theorem requires that citizens' votes be statistically independent of one another (Grofman 1978; Grofman and Feld 1988). That is, how one person votes should not be influenced by how others do. There is a large literature on Condorcet's jury theorem and statistical independence (Estlund et al. 1989; Ladha 1992; S. Berg 1993a, 1993b, 1996; Estlund 1994; Miller 1996; Kanazawa 1999).

[46] In very small groups, unless average competence is significantly better than random, the result of judgment-aggregation is middling, yielding a modest improvement over the competence of the average voter (Goodin 2003; Goodin and Estlund 2004).

The first of these suggestions (the direct assault on voter competence) is not supported by existing empirical research. Once again, there simply is not enough data to generate conclusions of this sort. That said, framing effects are the very sort of biases that should be of concern to the Condorcetian: they represent the possibility of a systematic bias that could quickly overwhelm the otherwise reliable epistemic capacities of citizens. As a result, such theories should be willing to dedicate substantial resources to preventing framing from undermining individual competence.

The second suggestion (the depleting effect of frames on the ranks of effective voters) is, interestingly enough, just the sort of thing that could be studied empirically. A large enough survey of the efficacy of framing in politics should be able to determine the extent to which we are, on average, susceptible to framing effects.[47] Assuming that it is in some way possible to estimate the number of individuals who frame political issues, it would then be possible to generate a hypothesis about the size of the effective electorate. In this way, we could evaluate whether framing effects really do violate the independence condition in a manner serious enough to challenge Condorcetian theories of democracy. Unfortunately, there have been no studies of this sort, and as a result, there does not seem to be any clear indication of whether such concerns are warranted.

Given the extent to which Condorcetian theories of democracy are dependent on the epistemic value of democracy, these theories should be highly sensitive to potential threats to individual political judgment. Even though empirical research is not conclusive here, Condorcetian theories seem obliged to dedicate very substantial resources to eliminating framing effects. Because for this account the consequences of poor decision making are so dire (the jury theorem predicts that individuals with worse than random competence will generate systematically incorrect decisions), Condorcetian theories ought to be highly receptive to empirical suggestions regarding ways to improve political judgment.

4.4.3 Correctness Theories

The mere existence of framing effects in politics poses problems for correctness theories of democracy, as they lead us to doubt the reliability of democratic decisions. Because these theories construe the value of

---

[47] Meta-analyses of empirical studies of framing effects have been conducted regarding other domains of human decision making (Kühberger 1998; Kühberger et al. 1999; Seburn 2001; Moxey et al. 2003; Woodside and Dubelaar 2003), but none have looked specifically at the efficacy of framing in politics. It would be instructive in the future if this sort of research were undertaken. As it stands right now, there are probably too few studies of political framing effects for such an analysis to be conclusive.

democracy as entirely reliant on its making correct judgments about politics, any evidence that democratic decision making is flawed will cause the correctness theorist considerable worry.

Because correctness theories claim that political decisions are only legitimate when they are substantively correct, evidence showing that individual voters are responsive to changes in the framing of political decisions should be taken as evidence that democracy is not a completely reliable mechanism for generating correct political decisions. Especially in cases where electoral decisions are made by a relatively small margin, the existence of any number of citizens whose votes are likely to have been swayed by frames will provide the correctness theorist with reason to doubt the legitimacy of those decisions. As a result, correctness theorists should be led to look far and wide for mechanisms capable of immunizing political judgment against the effects of framing.

Given the exacting epistemic standards that correctness theories place on voters, however, empirical proposals would have to effectively eliminate framing effects (or at least render them so small as to have a negligible influence on outcomes) in order to make such theories feasible. Indeed, correctness theories appear to demand an epistemically flawless electorate. In order for correctness theories to be plausible, then, it would seem that all citizens in a democracy must be responsive only to good reasons. Although it may be possible to develop mechanisms capable of eradicating the pernicious effects of framing, such mechanisms would likely come at considerable cost to society. Clearly, a whole litany of mechanisms would be required to improve democratic decision making, but it is not clear that it would be feasible to improve judgment to the level that is demanded by correctness theories.

CHAPTER FIVE

Institutional Implications

IN THIS CHAPTER, I illustrate some institutional implications of the behavioral approach to normative democratic theory. In the previous chapter, I laid out how various theories of democracy are affected by framing. I hope to have shown that all but the most minimalist theories of democracy must rely, at least to some extent, on claims regarding the reliability of citizens' judgment. Further, I hope it is clear that our susceptibility to framing poses a threat to any such claims. If this is the case, then any nonminimalist theory of democracy, in order to be feasible, ought to recommend institutional mechanisms geared toward improving the reliability of democratic decision making. In particular, I argue that such theories ought to endorse institutions capable of reducing the epistemically damaging effects of framing.

Because (as we have seen) particular theories of democracy place greater or lesser demands on the judgment of citizens (and are thus to a greater or lesser extent vulnerable to framing) different theories of democracy will be committed to different institutional arrangements. Theories of democracy that make few epistemic claims may be able to get away with relatively few judgment-improving devices, whereas fully epistemic theories seem to be committed to a whole host of institutional fixes. My aim in this chapter is not to specify which theories ought to endorse particular institutional arrangements. That would be tedious and overly contentious. Instead, I hope merely to present a menu of institutional options for ameliorating democratic decision making.

Some democratic theorists will undoubtedly have qualms about the specific recommendations outlined here, and some of these concerns may well be warranted.[1] I hope to have shown, however, that nonminimalist theories of democracy cannot take their epistemic claims about democracy for granted, and, if they are to propose strong moral reasons for endorsing democracy, they must be willing to dedicate significant resources to bolstering democratic decision making. As a result, this chapter is designed to present the options available to nonminimalist theories of democracy, but I will leave it to proponents of particular theories to choose from these options as they see fit.

---

[1] In particular, moral objections to review mechanisms (section 5.2.2) are likely to be widespread and perhaps (on some accounts) decisive.

5.1 POLITICAL SPEECH

The first set of institutional mechanisms designed to improve the epistemic value of democratic decision making concern the amount and diversity of political speech in a society. In particular, these initiatives are designed to ensure that there is a wide diversity of frames for political issues, a diversity that is fostered by a number of distinct and dissimilar political and media groups. By increasing the number of frames for political issues, it is hoped that the individual judgments of citizens will become less responsive to framing effects and more responsive to the substantive political issues at stake. If this is the case, then when these judgments are aggregated, collective decisions should do a better job of making correct judgments about politics.[2]

5.1.1 Competing Frames

Recently, empirical research into the effect of competition among frames[3] has led to a number of advances in our understanding of the psychological mechanisms that underlie our susceptibility to framing.[4] In particular, it has become apparent that certain qualities of frames, and not just their repetition, are central to their effectiveness.[5] Details of this sort will be important for the design of democratic institutions aimed at mitigating the effect of framing. Insofar as such research makes it possible to tailor measures to counteract specific characteristics of frames rather than exercising broad control over political speech, the amount of intervention in political speech and the costs associated with such intervention will decrease. This research, however, is still only in its infancy.

[2] The mechanisms outlined here will be particularly important for theories of democracy that have concerns about potential failures of judgment stemming from our being averse to losses (see sections 4.1.2 and 4.1.3). Such mechanisms aim to prevent the kind of monopoly over framing that could potentially exploit our tendency to overreact to losses.

[3] Competition—sometimes called "dual framing" (Bernstein et al. 1999)—refers to a condition in which individuals are exposed to more than one frame for a given issue. Each frame in turn emphasizes different elements of the decision problem. The general expectation here is that when competition obtains, framing will be less pernicious (Druckman 2001a, 2004).

[4] See, for example, work by Sniderman (Sniderman 2000; Sniderman and Theriault 2004; Sniderman and Levendusky 2007) and Druckman (Druckman and Nelson 2003; Druckman and Chong 2007; Druckman, Hennessy, et al. 2010).

[5] Tests of frame strength (Druckman and Chong 2007) are still rather crude (usually measured by the testimony of experimental subjects), but they do suffice to show that mere repetition of weak frames is often ineffective. Most interestingly, Berinsky and Kinder (2006) have argued that the ability of a frame to organize information into an effective story or narrative is central to its ability to sway individual opinions (Pennington and Hastie 1992; Hastie et al. 2002).

Currently, the dominant paradigm for empirical research into competition between frames remains that of political preference formation and consistency.[6] As a result, these findings can offer only limited evidence of the beneficial effects of competition on the reliability of judgments about political issues. These studies demonstrate that in many situations, competition between frames alters the effect of specific frames and seems to cause some individuals to weigh the appropriateness of competing frames against one another. This, I will assume, ought to have a beneficial effect on the ability of citizens to assess the strength of the reasons behind these frames. We need to be clear, however, that at this stage the epistemic advantages of competition are empirically unproven. That framing affects choice is clear, as is the fact that competition among frames alters the effect of frames, but there is as yet no direct evidence that this alteration in the effects of framing from competition results in better (or worse) political judgments (where these judgments are evaluated against independent standards of correctness). There is simply no data indicating whether the epistemic effect of competition among frames is ameliorative or is damaging. I take it to be, however, a plausible assumption that inducing individuals to consider alternative frames for an issue will lead to their providing a better assessment of the substantive questions involved, rather than merely being swayed by the particular description (the frame) they initially received.

The above assumption could be false: it could be the case that competition between frames leads individuals to make worse (or equally bad) decisions than they would under the influence of only one frame.[7] If this were so, however, then the prospects for reducing the pernicious effects of framing will be exceedingly bleak and the rational capacities of citizens would have to be compromised in startling and exceptional ways. If leading people to reframe issues by means of competition cannot improve the quality of their decision making, then very little will be capable of doing so. As a result, I hope that my assumption that competition between frames will—at least in some situations—lead to substantively better decision making will not strike readers as untenably optimistic.[8] Indeed, it seems that only the most pessimistic appraisal of human

[6] See especially Druckman (2004) and Druckman and Chong (2011) for instructive analyses of political responsiveness to preferences. Also, in "The Structure of Political Argument and the Logic of Issue Framing," Sniderman and Theriault (2004) measure the effect of competing frames for political issues against previously expressed political principles. Their research shows that competitive contexts lead to decisions that are more consistent with political principles than noncompetitive contexts.

[7] This could be the case, for example, if exposure to more than one frame resulted in confusion or decision-making paralysis. Although this may occur in extreme cases, it does not appear to be the norm.

[8] This is especially the case when one considers the documented effects of competition on the consistency and stability of preferences (Sniderman and Theriault 2004; Druckman

cognitive abilities (indeed, one that does not appear to be warranted by the existing literature) would object to it.

Assuming that, all other things being equal, competition between frames tends to improve the quality of decision making over what can be expected in noncompetitive settings, the promotion of competition should be a priority for anyone interested in bolstering the epistemic value of democracy. The existence of a large and diverse set of effective frames for political issues can in this way be expected to improve the epistemic quality of citizens' political judgment. Conversely, if only one or very few frames for political issues predominate, then we should expect, all other things being equal, political decision making to be relatively deficient. The most obvious political recommendation for counteracting framing effects will thus be the avoidance of situations in which citizens are exposed to only a small number of frames for political issues.

5.1.2 Monopolies and Oligopolies

If the above claims about the need for competition between frames are correct, then the most obvious threat to the epistemic value of democratic decision making will consist in the exertion of widespread control over issue frames. In particular, when one group has a monopoly or a small number of groups form an oligopoly that controls the dissemination of frames for political issues, the likelihood that frames will be in competition will be decreased. As a result, the concentration of control over the framing of issues ought to be avoided in democracies.

Unwanted concentrations of control over frames could be manifested in a number of ways. First, if there exists a small number of powerful political groups, these groups could be expected—whether deliberately or not—to curtail competition between frames. A second potential source of unwanted control concerns the number of individuals or groups that exert control over the media. The existence of monopolies or oligopolies in either politics or the media would seem to indicate, at least prima facie, that competition between frames would not suffice to improve the epistemic value of democratic decision making.

5.1.3 The Antitrust Analogy

A number of institutional mechanisms might be recommended in order to prevent the existence and dominance of framing monopolies or oligopolies. Just as mechanisms can be designed to ensure the existence of

and Chong 2007). These studies reveal that competitive contexts lead to preferences that are more consistent and that deviate less from choices made in a neutral decision setting.

effective competition between corporations in market settings, analogous mechanisms might be developed to promote effective competition
between frames in political settings. In both business and framing, the
intention is to bring about more competition, even when existing incentives may lead to its reduction. Fortunately, there are a number of pre-
existing institutional mechanisms that could be mobilized to prevent the
epistemically damaging effects of the monopolization of political frames.
In this way it is not necessary to propose radical changes to existing
political institutions and practices.[9]

Given the amount of controversy surrounding particular proposals
aimed at avoiding monopolies and oligopolies, my intention here will not
be to provide a convincing case for these reforms but rather simply to lay
out the epistemic arguments in favor of them. I use the model of antitrust
law—regulations designed to promote and protect economic competition
(O. Black 2005)—to highlight the fact that in both markets and politics
many benefits can only be expected under conditions of competition, but
those conditions are not always self-maintaining.

5.1.3.1 POLITICAL ANTITRUST DEVICES

The first class of proposals aimed at protecting the epistemic value of
political speech cover mechanisms designed to ensure the presence of a
large number of political groups capable of reframing issues and disseminating these frames throughout the voting population. In these cases, it
is understood that individuals in positions of political power have influence over the ways in which citizens come to understand and think about
political questions. To the extent that the manner in which they frame
issues serves to help determine the decisions of citizens, competition
between such individuals can be expected to increase the amount of competition between the frames they propose.

Multiparty Systems. So far, my discussion of framing monopolies
and oligopolies has been rather superficial. In particular, I have relied
on the notion of powerful political groups without being precise about
the specific form such groups may take.[10] The most obvious outlet for
power in democratic societies is the political party. Given the role of parties in most systems of democratic representation, political parties come

---

[9] Although the institutions described below are relatively familiar to North American
democratic systems, they are not subject to universal acclaim. In each case there are fairly
common objections to these proposals. Because most of these objections involve considerations not relevant to my study, I will deal with them only sparingly.

[10] The notion of a "political elite" serves a similarly amorphous role in the social scientific literature. For discussion of some of the problems involved in the use of this term, see
Zuckerman (1977); Parry (2008).

to wield a large amount of political influence.[11] Some of that power is manifested in the degree of control parties have over the dissemination of frames for political issues. More than individual politicians, political parties have an interest in refining and systematizing the content of political messages conveyed to the public. Given a party's desire to present a unified message across a whole field of candidates, it can be expected to dedicate significant resources to processes involved in identifying, selecting, and refining its favored frames for controversial political issues.[12] Similarly, they will also devote much of their considerable wherewithal to the dissemination and popularization of these frames. To a significant extent, then, we should expect political parties to exert control over frames for political issues within a democratic electorate.

Now, as I have claimed above, it seems likely that competition between frames will improve political judgment. Further, it also seems likely that competition between political parties will increase competition between frames. Because a single party has very little incentive to generate political frames that are in competition with one another, we should not expect political parties that hold a monopoly to encourage widespread competition between frames for political issues. As a result, the existence of only one political party cannot be expected to improve the epistemic value of democratic decision making—to say nothing of the other negative consequences of a single-party state. This is a significant epistemic reason, I think, to avoid the existence of single-party systems.

Similarly, the existence of a very small number of political parties will not significantly improve the reliability of the political judgment of citizens. Although parties that hold differing positions on a particular issue can—if they are competing with one another—be expected to generate competing frames regarding those issues, they should not be expected to generate competing frames for issues on which they either agree or remain silent.[13] Because individual parties establish positions on only a small subset of all possibly contentious political issues, a small number

[11] For a useful analysis of political parties from a social choice perspective, see Brennan and Hamlin (2000).

[12] This insight garnered much popular attention during the U.S. 2004 elections as a result of the publication of *Don't Think of an Elephant!* (Lakoff 2004).

[13] It should be clear that the epistemic benefits of competition between frames will only obtain in cases where political parties are actively competing. If political parties instead collude with one another rather than compete, no such benefits will result. That is, if political parties agree to take political issues off the table of discussion (e.g., in a cynical attempt to secure their own interests), competing frames for important political issues will be done away with and the judgment of citizens will be the worse for it. As a result, epistemic reasons concerning framing effects should incline us toward supporting political systems with large numbers of political parties, where those parties are engaged in vigorous competition on a whole range of issues.

of parties cannot be relied on to generate enough competition between frames for all important issues. Rather, opposing parties will generate competing frames only regarding the limited number of issues on which they explicitly disagree. Thus, if we want competition between frames for all or even the majority of important political issues, we require a diversity of political parties.[14]

It is sometimes true that within a political party internal competition can generate new political frames (as is sometimes the case with primary elections). However, given the remove at which such debates usually occur from the broader electorate and the high amount of agreement that normally characterizes members of the same political party, competition between such frames is not likely to have much of an effect on the epistemic reliability of citizen's judgment more generally.

As a result, if there are only a small number of political parties, then the epistemically beneficial effects of competition between frames will accrue only to a select number of issues. In order to ensure that competition between frames serves to improve political judgment across the whole range of political issues there must exist a wider diversity of political parties. Two- and perhaps even three-party oligopolies over frames are thus not likely to improve the decision making of citizens in a democracy.[15]

There are a number of plausible proposals for how to encourage the development of large numbers of viable political parties. I should admit, however, that it is not clear how many political parties would be required to substantially improve political decision making, or whether after some threshold the addition of more parties might cease to add to (or in fact decrease) the epistemic value of democratic decision making. I hope it is clear from the above, however, how a large group of political parties, each acting to reframe a diverse number of issues, can help to mitigate the epistemically pernicious effects of framing. In the next section I focus on one proposal aimed at increasing the number of competing political parties.

---

[14] Analyses from social choice theory support this claim as well. The widely influential median voter model (Congleton 2004) predicts that party platforms will tend to converge on the policy preferences of centrist voters. Over time, this will lead to political parties coming to resemble one another (Downs 1957).

[15] It might be claimed that on these grounds I should also be committed to the existence of epistemic reasons for opposing systems of simple majority voting (as contrasted with proportional representation schemes). Duverger's law (Duverger 1972) is often cited as showing that voting systems such as those found in the United States necessarily lead to a two-party system. I am unconvinced. Both Canada and India (there are other examples as well) use majority voting systems, and yet each have maintained a larger number of effective political parties. I should point out, however, that in cases where there is an entrenched two-party system, epistemic reasons would favor the use of proportional representation to break up the existing oligopoly. For an intriguing discussion of the status of Duverger's law, see Riker (1982b).

Barriers to Entry. As in the market case, one of the most effective ways to break up monopolies and oligopolies will be to introduce measures aimed at eliminating barriers to entry into competition. That is, institutional mechanisms are to be sought that can make it easier for individuals and groups to compete with established political parties. The most obvious barrier to entry into contemporary politics consists in the large financial costs associated with running a political campaign. Many of the costs associated with entering politics specifically concern the framing of political messages. Political parties dedicate enormous resources to developing, studying, and testing frames for political issues even before the expensive process of disseminating these frames begins.[16] As a result, in order to effectively compete with established political parties, massive financial reserves are required. Without enough funds, attempts at competition with established political parties are unlikely to succeed. So institutional mechanisms designed to reduce the amount of money required to compete in elections should be seen as having the potential to promote the epistemic value of the electoral process. If such mechanisms were to be successful, the costs—and therefore the risks—involved in entering into political competition would be reduced. If more political parties are able to enter politics, then we can expect more competition between frames for political issues.

In the United States various proposals to limit the amount of money involved in elections—usually called campaign finance reform—have met with very little success.[17] Most often, opponents criticize these proposals on the basis that such limitations would restrict political speech. Although I cannot go into these debates here, it should be noted that if the above claims are correct, then epistemic arguments could be mobilized to respond to such criticisms. For individuals who agree that making correct political decisions is an important aim of democracy, barriers to entry into political competition should represent important epistemic fetters to the reliability of democratic decision making.

5.1.3.2 Media Antitrust Devices

So far I have focused on the role of political parties in framing political issues in democratic societies. There are, however, other groups capable of creating and disseminating effective political frames, and they are able to do so (at least some of the time) independently of the influence of political parties. Most obviously, various media entities (e.g., newspapers,

[16] For an idea of the amount of money involved in American presidential campaigns, see *Financing the 2008 Election* (Magleby and Corrado 2011).

[17] For a compilation of some relevant documents and cases, see Corrado et al. (2005). For an analysis of the importance of the recent U.S. Supreme Court decision in *Citizens United v. Federal Election Commission*, see J. Cohen (2011).

radio and television broadcasters, and Internet content providers) have the ability to frame political issues and convey those frames to large portions of the population. Insofar as these entities can help to promote effective competition between frames for political issues, they too have the ability to bolster the political judgment of citizens.

As in the case of political parties, the primary threat to competition between frames for political issues will be the existence of a monopoly or oligopoly of control over media frames. The most obvious way in which such concentrations of power can come about result from the consolidation of media ownership in the hands of relatively few individuals or groups.

Media Consolidation. The existence of a large number of separate media entities seems to be the best way of ensuring widespread competition between media frames for political issues. In this way, the antitrust analogy is quite apt here. Mechanisms for breaking up corporate monopolies are well established in many countries, and the breakup of media monopolies and oligopolies usually falls within the jurisdiction of these mechanisms.[18] As a result, political institutions are already in existence that can help to increase competition between media frames.

I should pause, however, in order to consider a challenge to my claim that monopolies and oligopolies of media ownership will lead to the lack of competition between frames. It could be argued that individual media outlets, all owned by a single individual or corporation, might still propose and disseminate competing frames for political issues. It is possible that if a corporation were sufficiently motivated, it might produce a number of different frames that are in competition with one another. Such motivation, however, seems largely absent from market settings. Instead, the dictates of fiscal efficiency and profitability, at least in the long run, incline owners toward homogenizing the products of their media properties, thus decreasing the amount of competition between frames. As a result, the link between monopolies (or oligopolies) of ownership and monopolies (or oligopolies) of frames seems to be quite reliable.[19]

Media Independence. In a recent article, Jürgen Habermas (2006) engages with empirical research on the pathologies of political communication (including framing effects) in order to lay out two necessary conditions for the epistemic value of deliberative democracy. His concern

---

[18] For example, the 1984 antitrust divestiture of Bell Systems (also known as AT&T and Ma Bell) by the U.S. Department of Justice was an attempt to increase competition among telecommunications companies.

[19] For a description of this and related issues, see Delli Carpini (2005).

throughout this argument is the role of the media in preserving the reflexive character of the public sphere. These are his two conditions: "First, a self-regulating media system must maintain its independence vis-à-vis its environments while linking political communication in the public sphere with both civil society and the political center; second, an inclusive civil society must empower citizens to participate in and respond to a public discourse that, in turn, must not degenerate into a colonizing mode of communication" (Habermas 2006, 419). Habermas follows this with an account of how the media can undermine the functioning of the public sphere, either through the media's connections to political power or by being transformed into markets. In the former case, media institutions lose their independence by failing to sufficiently differentiate themselves from politics,[20] whereas in the latter case, the media's commodification of political coverage leads citizens to disengage from politics in a way that paralyzes the public sphere.[21]

Habermas here presents a rich and complex analysis of the role of the media within an epistemic theory of deliberative democracy. For our purposes, two points are most important. First, Habermas's claim that media power must remain distinct from political power is instructive for our understanding of competition between frames. In order to ensure the dissemination of a diversity of frames for political issues, we need to prevent media entities from becoming linked to particular political parties. Thus, not only do we need to prevent the existence of political monopolies and media monopolies, but we also need to prevent the existence of political-media oligopolies. Even if there are a number of political parties and a number of media entities, if the connections between them become too strong, then this will reduce the amount of effective competition that exists between frames. Thus, antitrust-style measures designed to ensure that the media is independent from political parties will conduce to the epistemic value of democratic decision making.

Second, Habermas's observation that market incentives can lead media entities to skew the manner in which they communicate political issues should lead us to consider the importance of public funding for media programs.[22] Habermas is particularly concerned about the negative

---

[20] Habermas's examples come from media developments in Italy (Padovani 2005) and coverage of the U.S. invasion of Iraq (Artz and Kamalipour 2005).

[21] For evidence of political disengagement, see Delli Carpini (2004); Lee (2005). For an account of how the commodification of the news leads to candidate-centered electoral politics, see Dalton (2006).

[22] Habermas's example of such skewed presentation is the "personalization of politics" (Habermas 2006, 423), the tendency of the media to substitute images of political candidates for treatment of political issues. We might understand this as the dominance of a certain kind of frame for political issues, one that tends to increase media profits.

influence of sustained economic pressure on the content of political journalism. In order to prevent this influence, antitrust mechanisms might be put to use in order to ensure the separation of the media from markets. In particular, insulating some elements of the media from market pressures would help to ensure a diversity of frames for political issues, a diversity that could be undermined by privatization. Insofar as market pressures can drive a number of media outlets to adopt similar programming structures and issue frames, independence of at least some media from the market serves to promote the epistemic value of democratic decision making.[23] Public media, then, have an important role to play in promoting the epistemic value of democracy.

5.1.4 The "Quality, Not Quantity" Objection

Taken together, the above arguments might make it seem as if the answer to the problem of framing effects (i.e., increase the number of frames) is too simple. If we pay no attention to the content of these frames, it may be claimed, this strategy will be ineffective. According to this criticism, more frames are not what we need; what we need are better frames. Further, it might be objected that, given the multifaceted nature of most controversial political issues, it will be neither feasible nor desirable to frame issues in every possible way. Because there is an almost unlimited number of frames—many of them redundant, incoherent, or crazed—for any given political issue, it seems as though the above strategy would result in a futile attempt to generate more and more frames. Given that there are practical limits to the number of frames that can be presented and cognitive limits to our capacity to understand them, it might appear that the strategy of diversifying frames is ultimately pointless.[24] At the very least, it appears that efforts to present more and more frames will, past a certain point, have diminishing epistemic value.

This criticism should lead us to question whether it is in fact more frames that we need. Could it be that we don't need more frames, we just need the right frames? If it were possible to identify the correct frame for a given political issue, then we could ignore the threat of media monopolies or political oligopolies and simply ensure that individuals were exposed

---

[23] It might be thought that this second claim is in tension with Habermas's requirement that the media remain independent of politics. For Habermas, however, there is a clear distinction between the core of the political system and the various channels of mediated communication. For our purposes, as long as it is possible to distinguish between the government that allocates public funding and the political party in power, this tension should not affect our understanding of the importance of competition between public and private media frames.

[24] Larry Bartels has formulated a version of this objection (Bartels 2003a, 2003b).

to the correct frames. The obvious difficulty here lies in identifying which frames for a political issue are normatively appropriate. As we saw earlier, Sunstein and Thaler's libertarian paternalism (Sunstein and Thaler 2008) proposes a welfarist standard for the evaluation of frames. It is not clear, however, why this standard and not some other (e.g., principles of justice) ought to serve as the appropriate standard for the evaluation of frames. Given this situation, is it possible to identify the set of normatively appropriate frames?

The Cognitivist Answer. One fairly straightforward way of responding to this question is to claim that the normatively appropriate frames are those whose dissemination would lead to political judgments that are substantively correct. As we have been operating under the assumption that, at least some of the time, there are independent standards against which we must evaluate the correctness of our judgments (see section 1.5.1 above), we might claim that we ought to disseminate just those frames that help individuals make judgments that accord with these standards.

Although this might at one level be a satisfying reply, it is not clear that it can provide any practical help for the design of political institutions. We can, for example, be committed to the existence of truth in politics without thereby believing that there is any legitimate mechanism for identifying such truths in a particular instance. It might be the case that we ought to circulate frames that will lead individuals to make correct political judgments, but—in the absence of a reliable and uncontroversial method for determining which frames will lead individuals to judge correctly—it seems likely that the only way to ensure that such frames are circulated is by attempting to disseminate as many frames as possible.

The Complexity Answer. Another way of responding to this difficulty would be to claim that although it is not possible to identify which frames will lead directly to correct political decisions, we can limit the dissemination of frames to the smallest set capable of conveying all the information relevant for that decision. On this model, we ought to select frames that convey as much of the complexity of the political issue at hand as possible, thereby obviating the need to have open-ended competition between frames.[25] If only one frame or a small number of frames is capable of conveying all of the relevant details of the political issue at hand, then there is no reason to burden the public with more frames than are necessary. By packing complexity into a small number of frames, we

[25] I am grateful to Ange-Marie Hancock for this suggestion. For her treatment of media framing, see Hancock (2004).

might reduce the amount of competition required to generate good political decisions.

Unfortunately, this reply falls short in many of the same ways that the cognitivist's does: although it may be the case that some small number of frames are capable of capturing all of the epistemically relevant information in a given political decision, there does not appear to be any non-question-begging means of identifying such frames in actual cases. In particular, it isn't clear how one could go about ascertaining how much detail (and what kind of detail) is relevant for a given political decision. So, once again it seems as if the best way to ensure that all the relevant information circulates is to encourage the dissemination of as many frames as possible.

The Liberal Answer. A more familiar reply to this question involves claiming that even if we are—at some level—committed to the existence of truth about political issues, we cannot expect individuals to agree about what this truth is in any particular instance.[26] Reasonable persons, it may be said, are likely to disagree about which political decision is correct and will thus also disagree about which frame is normatively appropriate.[27] If this is correct, then the liberal reply will advocate disseminating all and only those frames that could be endorsed by reasonable persons. Thus, a political liberal will advocate restricting the dissemination of frames to reflect standards of reasonableness. This will eliminate some frames—such as the crazed and the incoherent—though it is not clear how many.[28] Therefore, the best solution, both from an epistemic and a moral standpoint, would seem to be to provide anyone who has a reasonable perspective on an issue with some ability (either directly or through representatives) to disseminate a frame aimed at persuading others of the correctness of her view. Although it may be tempting in any given instance to think that, in light of one's firmly held political convictions, some particular frame for a political issue ought to prevail to the

---

[26] For an account of why this might be the case, see John Rawls's description of the burdens of judgment (Rawls 1993, 54–58).

[27] Given the existence of widespread reasonable political disagreement, not only regarding individual political questions but also political principles, we should expect this disagreement to extend to normative standards for the evaluation of frames. Further, even if we were to assume that there might be reasonable agreement about the correct decision, there could still be disagreement about which frame would best serve to bring about that decision.

[28] It might be the case that Rawls's supposition that "a reasonable comprehensive doctrine does not reject the essentials of a democratic regime" (Rawls 1993, xvii) can be used to pare down the set of reasonable frames for political issues. This seems plausible, but I am unsure how one would go about implementing this at a policy level.

exclusion of all others, this approach seems to be ruled out for standard Rawlsian reasons concerning the nature of public reason (Rawls 1993).

As a result, it appears that in practice, a liberal approach to the dissemination of political frames will be indistinguishable from the more indiscriminate approach outlined above. Because liberals would require a large amount of competition between frames—substantially more than is currently the case—the antitrust strategies outlined above should seem quite attractive. The only difference would involve how the liberal would react to unreasonable frames (Rawls 1993, 64n).

5.2 INSULATING STRATEGIES

What if the proposals sketched above do not sufficiently reduce the pernicious effects of framing? If it is not the case that exposing individuals to more than one frame improves the political judgment of citizens, then, at least in certain circumstances, we might doubt the reliability of democratic decision making. One strategy for increasing the epistemic value of democracy is to establish institutions within democratic societies designed to insulate democratic outcomes from epistemic mistakes. In general, the idea here is to use institutional means to prevent a certain class of questions from being decided in a manner that is deemed to be inappropriate. Less abstractly, this means taking many political questions off the table. In this way, democratic outcomes (i.e., the laws and policies that are actually enforced) are insulated from flawed decision making (e.g., in referendums or laws passed by a legislature).[29]

5.2.1 Constitutions

In many democratic societies the protection of a system of basic rights is deemed too important to be subject to the possibility of being revoked by conventional democratic means.[30] Thus, it is common to see a system of basic rights enshrined in a constitution and thereby removed from the set of political issues currently up for grabs. One way of interpreting

---

[29] The notion of an insulating strategy is adapted from the work of Jolls and Sunstein (2006), who contrast this approach with debiasing. Clearly education (described below in section 5.3) counts as an instance of debiasing, but the proposals developed above (section 5.1) blur the distinction between insulation and debiasing.

[30] Societies differ in terms of the means required to alter these basic rights. Legal entrenchment, referendum procedures, supermajority rules, and various slowing-down mechanisms provide different strategies for insulating basic rights from normal electoral decision-making procedures. In what follows, I will not distinguish between these various means.

constitutionalism of this sort is as an attempt to ensure the epistemic value of democracy.[31] Given that we attach such great importance to decisions regarding basic rights, even if we cannot ensure that democratic decisions are substantively correct, we can protect democratic outcomes by preventing a certain class of particularly bad political decisions from ever coming to pass. In this way, the democratic system is epistemically improved: we are convinced of the correctness of certain judgments about rights (e.g., that they are universally held), so we ensure that citizens do not collectively err by undermining these rights.

Even if we construe constitutions in this way, however, it is unclear whether writing a bill of rights and having it legally entrenched can actually prevent poor democratic decisions from becoming poor democratic outcomes. Constitutions do not interpret themselves, and policies do not arrest politicians. In order for a constitution to effectively insulate democratic outcomes from faulty decision making, there must be some institutional mechanism available that is capable of identifying constitutionally illegitimate decisions and preventing them from being enacted.[32] Citizens and legislators are all too capable of ignoring the unconstitutionality of proposed legislation, and constitutions as such seem incapable of saving us from our own bad decisions.[33] This is where institutions of review come into play.[34]

5.2.2 Review

On the view I am presenting here, mechanisms for reviewing the collective decisions of citizens—decisions produced either directly (by means of plebiscites) or indirectly (by means of representatives)—are to be interpreted primarily as a kind of quality control on democratic decision making. Decisions are vetted by an entity within the political system (broadly construed), and those that are found to be either substantively incorrect or otherwise deficient are, in some way or another, blocked

---

[31] This is a fairly schematic way of understanding the relationship between a system of basic rights and democratic decision making. For a fuller account of this relationship that focuses on both moral and pragmatic constraints, see *Between Facts and Norms* (Habermas 1996).

[32] On the many difficulties involved in constitutional interpretation, see the work of David Lyons (1987, 1993a, 1993b, 1993c).

[33] Precommitment strategies have received a great deal of attention and criticism in both the philosophical and social scientific literature. For the most influential statement and critique of such strategies, see the work of Jon Elster (1984, 2000).

[34] For a review of challenges to the legitimacy of constitutionalism in general, see the work of Andrei Marmor (2007)

from becoming law.[35] In cases where review is conjoined to a constitution or system of rights, the result is most commonly some form of judicial review.

5.2.2.1 JUDICIAL REVIEW

There exists a massive and rich literature on the vexed relationship between democracy and judicial review.[36] Innumerable claims and controversies are relevant in assessing the legitimacy of judicial review, but I cannot deal with all of them here. Instead, in what follows, I will concern myself with one small part of this literature, focusing on the potential epistemic value of judicial review.[37] In particular, I will investigate whether judicial review can be expected to increase the epistemic reliability of democracy. This possibility, when construed in conjunction with empirical data on framing effects and other cognitive pathologies, opens up a slightly different way of assessing the case for judicial review.[38]

In order to structure my analysis of the potential epistemic value of judicial review, I will make use of a recent statement of the case against judicial review by Jeremy Waldron (2006). In "The Core of the Case against Judicial Review,"[39] Waldron argues that outcome-related reasons[40] to endorse judicial review are inconclusive, whereas process-related rea-

---

[35] There are potential differences both in the criteria that might be used to evaluate decisions and in the means used to block them. Review criteria could include moral standards, procedural requirements, or, most commonly, a requirement of fit with a system of rights. Further, review systems could block the enactment of decisions; they could reinterpret the meaning of a decision; they could amend the decision; or they could demand that citizens amend their decision. In each of these cases, however, the review mechanisms are expected to improve on initial electoral decisions.

[36] The most prominent figures in this literature are John Hart Ely (1980, 1996), Ronald Dworkin (1996, 2006b), and Jeremy Waldron (see below). There are, however, are a great many others as well.

[37] Although this is not a familiar way of formulating the role of judicial review within democracy, it is not intended to be altogether novel. Rather, many instrumentalist justifications of judicial review could easily be recast as assertions about the epistemic value of these procedures. Thus, John Hart Ely's famous claim that judicial review is "representation-reinforcing" (Ely 1980) might be interpreted as a claim about the epistemic reliability of the judiciary's judgment on issues of political participation and free speech. In this way, some of the most familiar claims about the instrumental importance of judicial review can be construed as arguments in favor of its epistemic value.

[38] A related argument has already been presented with regard to evidence of political ignorance among voters (Somin 2004).

[39] Versions and precedents of this argument can be found in many of Waldron's earlier writings (1992, 1993a, 1993b, 1998a, 1998b, 1998c, 1999a, 1999b, 1999c, 2002, 2004a, 2004b).

[40] I understand outcome-related reasons to include those instrumental goods that judicial review is expected to produce. Most important among these are substantively correct decisions regarding controversial questions about rights.

sons[41] unambiguously support majoritarian democracy unencumbered by review mechanisms.[42] He concludes that in cases where democratic institutions are functioning relatively well we ought to oppose judicial review.[43] Waldron claims, essentially, that there is no compelling reason to think that a group of judges will do a better job of making decisions regarding controversial questions of individual rights than will a well-functioning legislature.

Waldron's argument does not proceed on the basis of framing effects or any other cognitive pathology.[44] Instead, his argument against the value of judicial review proceeds on the basis of general limitations to adjudicative practices (Fuller 1978; Hart et al. 1994) and various institutional constraints that might reduce the quality of judicial decision making concerning rights.[45] Given these drawbacks, Waldron argues that there is no compelling reason to allow unelected judges to exert veto power over legislation passed by democratically elected representatives.

I propose to adopt Waldron's way of structuring the debate over judicial review. In particular, I will concede that the burden of proof ought to lie with those who would propose mechanisms of judicial review. Further, I also follow Waldron in assuming that the positive case for judicial review must rely on outcome-related (i.e., epistemic) reasons. I will

[41] It is important to note that Waldron's criticism will only have traction with those who agree that democracy has procedural (what Waldron calls process-related) value. Thus, stability or correctness theorists will be unmoved by Waldron's argument unless they can be convinced that judicial review negatively influences the outcomes of democratic decision making (i.e., stability or substantively correct decisions).

[42] My concern in what follows is primarily with what Waldron would view as strong, rights-oriented, a posteriori, specialized judicial review (Waldron 2006, 1353–1359), although analogous claims could be made regarding other forms as well. For a discussion of review mechanisms that are not necessarily oriented toward the protection of individual rights, see the next section.

[43] There is a complication here regarding whether ours may be what Waldron calls a "non-core case" (Waldron 2006, 1359–1369). In particular, it might be thought that our susceptibility to framing effects (and our bounded rationality in general) prevents us from meeting his requirement that society has "democratic institutions in reasonably good working order" (Waldron 2006, 1346) and that, as a result, his criticism of judicial review ought not apply to our case. I take it to be evident that Waldron intends his "core cases" to involve individuals not terribly different from the ones in many existing democratic societies and thus that we should not expect framing effects to invalidate the above assumption. I will therefore assume that our susceptibility to framing effects does not prevent democratic institutions from working reasonably well, by Waldron's standards.

[44] I am also importing the language of "epistemic value" into his argument, as Waldron distinguishes only between outcome- and process-related reasons.

[45] Waldron is particularly critical of three sets of claims often advanced in favor of the instrumental value of judicial review: the court's orientation to particular cases, the court's reliance on the text of a bill of rights, and the court's ability to state reasons for its decisions (Waldron 2006, 1379–1386).

argue that judicial review, if it is justifiable at all, will be so in spite of its countermajoritarian procedures and because of its epistemic value: judicial review can be reconciled with democracy only insofar as it serves to improve the decisions of democracies.[46]

When considered in light of data on cognitive biases, there are a number of reasons why we should expect judicial review to be epistemically valuable. In particular, we should expect judicial review to have an epistemic advantage over electoral decision making for reasons pertaining to (1) the selection of justices, (2) the design of court procedures, and (3) the resources available to justices. For these reasons, members of a supreme court can be expected to make judgments that have a significantly lower likelihood of falling prey to framing effects and other biases. Judges should not, on these grounds, be expected to be entirely immune from mistakes, but decisions made by a panel of such judges should be less prone to cognitive biases than decisions made by citizens more generally. Thus, in allowing a judicial panel to review and strike down legislation, it is possible to prevent bad decisions (e.g., decisions resulting from our susceptibility to framing effects) from being enforced. If judges in these instances exercise sound judgment, they can help to ensure that a democracy's enacted policies are substantively good ones.

First among these reasons, the procedures involved in selecting justices provides for the possibility of reducing the pernicious effects of framing and other cognitive pathologies. Because supreme court justices are usually selected from a larger set of judges,[47] who are selected from a larger set of lawyers, who are selected from a larger set of law school students, who are selected from a larger set of college students, who are selected from a larger set of young people, we have ample opportunity to implement selection procedures designed to pick out individuals that meet certain evaluative standards.[48] If, as part of each of these selection

---

[46] This is not an uncontroversial claim. John Rawls, for example, defended judicial review on the grounds that a supreme court, among other things, serves as an important exemplar of public reason (Rawls 1993, 235–240). Although I do not doubt that a supreme court could serve such a function, I do not see how—in the absence of its epistemic value—that function alone could legitimate judicial review: it is only insofar as the decisions of a supreme court lead to good outcomes that it could serve as an exemplar of public reason.

[47] The recent appointment of Justice Elena Kagan to the U.S. Supreme Court counts as an exception to this claim (there are others as well).

[48] It could be objected that it is legal judgment and not political judgment that is selected for in such processes. Further, it might be claimed that eliminating biases in legal judgment may not necessarily eliminate biases in political judgment. If we are interested in improving the political judgment of citizens with regard to controversial issues of rights, then—unless it is the case that legal judgment, when conjoined to a system of rights, effectively tracks political judgment—existing selection processes might not reliably improve democratic decision making about rights.

procedures, we evaluate candidates for their insusceptibility to cognitive biases, then we would have grounds to expect better cognitive performances from supreme court justices.[49]

Second, legal procedures can be designed to reduce the effect of various cognitive pathologies.[50] Many of the most familiar court procedures can serve as effective means of counteracting the effects of framing: formal discovery procedures, the hearing of arguments in an adversarial setting, the filing of amicus briefs by outside parties, and the drafting of a number of opinions by clerks. All of these can be expected to ensure that justices are exposed to a number of different frames for a particular issue. Such decision-making procedures provide cognitive advantages not available to the average voter. As a result, we should expect supreme court justices to be significantly less prone to framing effects.

Third, and most important, the many and extensive resources available to judges ought to afford them epistemic advantages that are well beyond the reach of most citizens. In particular, providing justices with large amounts of time and financial resources allows them to dedicate themselves to the task of good decision making in a way that is very different from situation of the average citizen. Very few people in democratic societies have the wherewithal to dedicate much of their labor to ensuring that they make correct decisions about controversial issues of rights.[51] Justices, however, have at their disposal not just their own labor but that of clerks and various other assistants as well. Given this, it seems quite reasonable that justices should be capable of avoiding many errors that most other citizens do not.[52]

---

[49] Even in the absence of dedicated tests for cognitive biases, it is possible to gauge epistemic performance in more indirect ways. For example, if behavioral law continues to increase in stature, it may eventually become part of a standard legal education. If this is the case and if we assume (see section 5.3 below) that education can mitigate cognitive pathologies, then we would have reason to expect someone who excelled in law school to avoid many cognitive biases.

[50] For examples, see *Debiasing through Law* (Jolls and Sunstein 2006) and the articles compiled in *Behavioral Law and Economics* (Sunstein 2000a), especially Sunstein and Ullmann-Margalit (2000); McCaffery et al. (2002).

[51] For clear articulations of the problems stemming from rational ignorance among voters, see Hardin (2009) and Somin (2010).

[52] It is important to note that if the epistemic advantages outlined above really are effective, then we might be obliged to provide them to citizens in general. In particular, if it is the case that the provision of adequate time and financial resources (and specialized education as well) are necessary to ensure reliable political decision making, then epistemic theories of democracy should demand that all citizens be provided with these resources. Some advantages, however, (e.g., the provision of clerks) will be impossible to provide to everyone. To this extent, even if all citizens were provided with the resources necessary to improve their decision making, we might still expect judicial review to serve a valuable epistemic role. For

I hope that the above reasons serve to give an indication of some positive reasons why a supreme court may contribute epistemic value to democracy. In particular, I hope that these reasons show how justices, by virtue of their position as justices, can be expected to avoid many common cognitive biases. Before moving on, however, I need to respond to two empirical objections to my claims. First, Cass Sunstein and his coauthors (Sunstein, Schkade, et al. 2006) have documented patterns of ideological voting among federal judges that may be taken to indicate that judicial decision making is epistemically unreliable.[53] Second, a different study (Guthrie et al. 2001) has produced evidence that judges are susceptible to some of the most familiar cognitive biases.[54]

Each of these studies might be taken as empirical support for Waldron's claim that judicial decision making is unlikely to be any better than citizen decision making. I think that this would be a mistake. In response to evidence that judges vote ideologically (i.e., they tend to toe the party line of the president who appointed them), it should be pointed out that ideological voting does not necessarily mean that panels of partisan judges will make poor decisions. Although it is disappointing that so many judges have predictable political patterns, much more research would be required to show that such patterning, when taken together, leads to substantively incorrect decisions.[55]

Similarly, research demonstrating that judges are susceptible to some cognitive biases might be disappointing, but it should not lead us to think that the decisions of a supreme court will not serve to improve the reliability of democratic decision making.[56] The studies cited above

---

an account of how resource constraints can undermine democratic decision making, see J. Cohen and Rogers (1983, 47–73).

[53] This study tracked voting patterns of U.S. federal judges to determine if the decisions of Democratic and Republican appointees differed systematically along party lines. They found that in some areas, though not all, patterns of ideological voting are present. See also Sunstein (1999, 2005c); Sunstein and Viscusi (2002); Sunstein, Schkade, et al. (2004).

[54] This study is based on survey evidence from U.S. federal magistrate judges. It documents their susceptibility to five separate cognitive biases. Although these judges did seem to exhibit anchoring, hindsight, and egocentric biases roughly akin to the rest of the population, they were less susceptible to the effects of framing and the representativeness heuristic. See also Viscusi (1999, 2001); Guthrie et al. (2002, 2005); Robbennolt (2002); Hersch and Viscusi (2004).

[55] Further, because so much voting behavior in democracies is clearly partisan, it is not the case that judicial review would have to be completely nonpartisan in order to improve the decision making of citizens.

[56] In this regard, it is interesting to compare the Guthrie, Rachlinski, and Wistrich study with the expansive empirical literature on jury decision making. Although, as the authors point out, such comparisons are not unproblematic (Guthrie et al. 2001, 816–818), it seems that judges still do better than jurors. See, for example, MacCoun (1989); Pennington and

are of a piece with results concerning other kinds of putative experts.[57] Research on lawyers, physicians, economists, and any number of other professional decision makers has demonstrated that expertise does not insulate individuals from falling prey to cognitive biases. It is important, however, that many of the cognitive advantages cited above (especially numbers 2 and 3) do not rely on the expertise of judges qua experts. I don't particularly care if judges, when filling out surveys at conferences, fall prey to cognitive biases. I care whether they fall prey to biases when they are writing their judicial decisions. The epistemic advantages alluded to above apply to judges in their role as, and in the institutional setting of, members of the supreme court. It would be nice if (and I think it is possible that) selection processes can produce a group of judges who do not fall prey to cognitive illusions. But even if justices are no better than the rest of us when filling out a survey, the institutional backdrop against which they do their jobs provides them with important epistemic advantages that should allow them to avoid many cognitive mistakes that would otherwise negatively influence democratic decision making about rights.

5.2.2.2 Risk Review

It should be noted that, from the standpoint of institutional design, there is nothing sui generis about decisions concerning rights. If the above epistemic argument is accepted, then it might be possible to argue for the review of democratic decision making, not against a system of rights but against other normative standards for good decision making. If we are concerned about the ability of democratic decisions to track the truth about political issues, and if not all political questions are issues of rights (at least not on their face), then it seems that we should be willing to countenance the possibility of establishing review mechanisms designed to improve democratic decision making concerning other issues as well.

It will be helpful here to focus on a particular example: take risk regulation. For some time now empirical researchers have documented numerous predictable failures in the way in which most individuals and groups manage risk.[58] It has been shown that we often misjudge risk: we underestimate certain kinds of dangers (e.g., from obesity and sun exposure), and overestimate others (e.g., from plane crashes and terrorist

---

Hastie (1992); Hastie et al. (2002); McCaffery et al. (2002); Sunstein and Viscusi (2002); Hersch and Viscusi (2004); A. Smith and Greene (2005).

[57] For an insightful account of the complexities surrounding the study of expert judgment, see Jeffrey Rachlinski, "Cognitive Errors, Individual Differences, and Paternalism" (2006). See also Neale and Northcraft (1986); Shrader-Frechette (1995); D. Koehler et al. (2002); Menand (2005); Tetlock (2005).

[58] For example, see the work of Posner (2004) and Sunstein (2009b).

attacks). These kinds of errors can sometimes lead to great losses, injury, and even death. Given this situation, shouldn't we seek to insulate democratic outcomes from poor democratic decision making concerning risk?

Recently, a number of prominent thinkers have advanced proposals in this vein: Stephen Breyer (now associate justice of the U.S. Supreme Court) recommended the creation of a federal board of experts located within the executive to assess and rationalize the risk policies of different branches of government (Breyer 1993, 55–81); Cass Sunstein (now administrator of the Office of Information and Regulatory Affairs) has defended a technocratic approach to environmental risk regulation (Sunstein 2002, 54–77); and Richard Posner (judge on the Seventh Circuit of the U.S. Court of Appeals) proposed the creation of a "Center for Catastrophic-Risk Assessment and Response" to improve regulation of unlikely but potentially cataclysmic events (Posner 2004, 216–244). Although none of these proposals would establish a mechanism of review with the same scope or power as the U.S. Supreme Court, there is, in principle, no reason why there could not be a formal review mechanism that sought to eliminate bad democratic decisions regarding risk.[59]

Any such proposal for risk review of democratic legislation would be enormously controversial. Some would claim that it is a *reductio* of the entire notion that we should attempt to increase the epistemic reliability of democratic decision making by means of review mechanisms. Others, however, will claim that such proposals could save millions (or perhaps billions) of lives and should be given due consideration. Some of this disagreement arises as a result of the difficulties involved in identifying experts in the field of risk assessment,[60] but more of it stems from concerns about threats to the legitimacy of democratic rule. Such controversies thus represent deep divides in democratic theory: in many cases

---

[59] Currently, in the United States, the National Environmental Policy Act (NEPA) serves as a very weak form of environmental risk review. Under the provisions of this act (42 U.S.C. 4321 et seq.), all agencies of the U.S. federal government must adhere to a set of procedural requirements aimed at publicizing any adverse environmental consequences of actions undertaken by these agencies. By making such consequences public, it is expected that federal decision makers will be led to make choices that better protect the environment. I call this act a form of risk review because one of its aims is to improve the quality of our judgments about risks to the environment. I call this a *very weak* form of risk review, however, because it does not require that the resulting decisions be made on environmental grounds. Instead, once all the required procedural steps have been taken and the relevant environmental impacts have been publicized, federal agencies are free to make their judgment on whatever basis they deem appropriate. This act thus serves as an indirect means of improving decision making. The form of risk review I envision above, by virtue of being substantive rather than procedural, is far stronger and more direct. For a comprehensive explanation of the law and policy governing environmental risk, see Revesz (2008).

[60] For an indication of the depths of these disagreements, see Kristin Shrader-Frechette's review (2006) of Cass Sunstein's *Laws of Fear* (2005b).

they reflect disagreements between procedural and epistemic theories of democracy. To that extent, it seems unlikely that resolving empirical questions about expertise will do much to address these disagreements.[61]

I hope it is clear, however, that many of the same epistemic arguments that can be used to justify systems of judicial review could be used to motivate more radical kinds of review as well. To the extent that we worry about the quality of our political judgment, we ought to be willing to countenance a whole litany of institutional means of shoring-up democratic decision making. Although it may indeed be the case that risk review carries too high a procedural price, epistemic concerns about the reliability of democratic decision making require that insulating strategies such as these at least be considered.[62]

5.3 EDUCATION

There is one very important strategy that I have yet to discuss. Perhaps the most obvious way to go about increasing the reliability of democratic decision making in the face of cognitive pathologies like framing effects is to try to eliminate them through the education of citizens. As we are interested in ascertaining whether it is feasible to attain the standards of competence set by various theories of democracy, the costs associated with particular proposals will be of central importance for this analysis. In the case of education, it should be possible to incorporate programs aimed at training all citizens to avoid cognitive errors within existing or expanded structures of public education. This will require only minimal alteration of existing institutions and moderate expense. Further, such educational programs would likely benefit citizens in a number of distinct ways extending well beyond the political realm.

---

[61] In particular, liberal theories of democracy will have problems with risk review. Under Rawls's understanding of the limits of political justification (Rawls 1993), it is difficult to see how the decisions of such an entity could be presented within the narrow scope of public reason. I cannot argue here for this conclusion, but it seems likely that—regardless of their stance on judicial review—consistent Rawlsian liberals will ultimately be unable to endorse a strong system of risk review.

[62] David Estlund claims that a general acceptability requirement on political justification effectively rules out invidious comparisons (e.g., claims that political knowledge travels with some other demographic characteristic) of the sort required to identify and empower political experts. He claims that it is always the case that someone could legitimately and decisively object to an expert's putative authority. Although it is not clear that mechanisms of review amount to the endorsement of an expert's political authority, this sort of objection might be mobilized to reject many forms of judicial or risk review. See Estlund (2008, chap. 11, "Why Not an Epistocracy of the Educated?").

Ridding decisions of framing effects could confer diverse advantages on citizens. These citizens can thus be expected to want to improve their decision making. Consider this: if education can eliminate framing, then we might expect individuals with proper training to make better health-care decisions,[63] have more coherent preferences,[64] be better stock market investors,[65] save more for retirement,[66] manage risks more efficiently,[67] be more responsible gamblers,[68] and make better professional judgments.[69] These are all good things, and it would seem to be incumbent on governments to provide these advantages to their citizens. The most important question, then, is whether proposals to eliminate framing effects through education are likely to succeed. There is, however, surprisingly little empirical evidence directly addressing this possibility. Much evidence documents the effects of educating individuals about other cognitive biases, but even this research is generally inconclusive.[70] Education and training seem to reduce some biases[71] but are ineffective in other cases.[72]

[63] On framing effects in health care, see McNeil, et al. (1982); Redelmeier and Shafir (1995); Bernstein et al. (1999); Wills (1999); Armstrong et al. (2002); Moxey et al. (2003).

[64] On the problems associated with preference reversals, see the articles compiled in *The Construction of Preference* (Lichtenstein and Slovic 2006).

[65] Here, see the work of Richard Thaler and his many coauthors (Tversky and Thaler 1990; Bernartzi and Thaler 1995; Thaler, Tversky, et al. 1997; Kahneman, Knetsch, et al. 2000a).

[66] See research on frames for 401(k) plans (Madrian and Shea 2001; Bernartzi and Thaler 2004; Sethi-Iyengar et al. 2004).

[67] For example, framing can negatively affect women's perception of their risk of breast cancer (Meyerowitz and Chaiken 1987; Lipkus et al. 2001; Elmore and Gigerenzer 2005).

[68] For an example of how framing can lead to bad gambles, see a recent analysis of game show decision making (Post et al. 2008).

[69] For an insightful account of how costly cognitive biases in professional judgment can persist for long periods of time, see Thaler and Sunstein's review (2004) of *Moneyball* (Lewis 2003).

[70] The literature on debiasing (Fischhoff 1982; Weinstein and Klein 2002; Jolls and Sunstein 2006) provides some hope for efforts such as these, but also some doubt. For a broad review of the relevant literature, see Baruch Fischhoff's "Heuristics and Biases in Application" (2002, 747–748).

[71] Confirmation bias (i.e., the tendency to interpret ambiguous or contradictory evidence so as to support an established hypothesis) can sometimes be avoided by warning individuals of this tendency (Highhouse and Bottrill 1995). Stereotype threat (i.e., the tendency to underperform when one's performance will serve to confirm an existing social stereotype) can sometimes be reduced by informing individuals about the procedures involved in measuring performance (Kang and Banaji 2006).

[72] Hindsight bias (i.e., the tendency of our ex post judgments to overestimate the ex ante probabilities of events that we know to have occurred) is particularly resistant to debiasing attempts. See, for example, Christensen-Szalanski and Willham (1991); Kamin and Rachlinski (1995); Sanna, Schwarz, and Small (2002); Sanna, Schwarz, and Stocker (2002); Sanna and Schwarz (2003).

Various debiasing strategies have met with some limited success, but no approach serves to eliminate all (or even most) biases.[73]

Further, education programs that train individuals to deal with cognitive biases over long periods of time have yielded only preliminary and ambiguous data (Fischhoff 2002, 747). Although much work has been done in designing curricula aimed at eliminating cognitive biases (Beyth-Marom and Dekel 1983; Baron and Brown 1991), it is still not clear how effective such programs will be. Incorporating the study of judgmental biases into more conventional critical thinking programs holds out promise for reducing the negative effects of these biases.[74] Treating framing effects and other cognitive biases as akin to logical fallacies would allow educators to improve decision making within existing programs of study. There is, unfortunately, little empirical data available to quantify the success of these programs.

Still, public education programs aimed at training people to avoid biases in their judgment have a number of advantages over the other strategies discussed in this chapter. Unlike mechanisms designed to increase the number of competing frames for political issues, educational initiatives hold the possibility of conveying epistemic benefits that extend well beyond democratic decisions. As a result, the costs associated with such programs would be easier to justify, given the range of possible good outcomes. Also, unlike systems of review, the procedural costs associated with educative solutions are very low. Training people to improve their decision making does not appear to pose any threat to the legitimacy of democratic government, nor does it require us to radically alter the structure of existing political institutions.

That said, public education programs do carry some costs. Such programs can be financially expensive, and they do require some deference to expertise. The individuals who design educational curricula aimed at improving our decision making have some degree of control over the contents of these programs and thus over the end results. Therefore, the details of such proposals are not uncontroversial. Also, given the current scarcity of reliable data on these programs, we should expect many false starts and dead ends. Further, education programs will likely take a very long time before they have any appreciable effects. For these reasons, education should not be viewed as a quick or certain fix to epistemic worries about democratic decision making. Such proposals are in many respects, however, the most plausible means of addressing epistemic concerns about democratic decision making.

[73] For debiasing techniques targeted to specific legal settings, see Babcock et al. (1997); Rachlinski (2003); A. Smith and Greene (2005).

[74] The work of Jonathan Baron (1998, 2000; Bazerman, Baron, et al. 2001; Baron 2005) is particularly impressive in this regard.

Conclusion

IN THIS WORK, I have tried to demonstrate that a behavioral approach to democratic theory—one that rejects the rational actor model of decision making in favor of a picture of choice informed by empirical psychology—can yield important theoretical results. In order to do this, I have focused on the phenomenon of framing effects and its relevance to normative theories of democracy. I hope to have generated two results that will validate the behavioral approach. The first concerns democratic theories at the minimalist end of my spectrum. The second result applies to theories that place epistemic demands on the judgment of citizens.

First, the fact that minimalist theories of democracy—those that make few if any demands on the judgment of citizens—can ignore the phenomenon of framing effects itself reveals the limitations of such theories. Purely procedural theories of democracy, by virtue of the fact that they disregard outcomes, are unaffected by the analysis of framing effects that I have presented here. Such theories do not see pathologies that can afflict human decision making as relevant to our understanding of the role and importance of democratic government. In refusing to acknowledge the importance of good decision making for the proper functioning of democracy, these theories limit themselves to very thin procedural grounds for recommending democracy. Although the procedural values at issue here are not insignificant, I hope it will be agreed that they can provide only weak moral reasons for supporting democratic government.

Stability theories of democracy propose a similarly weak endorsement of democracy. I hope to have shown that the kind of stability proposed by an austere stability theory is normatively suspect in a way that should lead us to question whether it can provide us with genuine reasons for supporting democratic arrangements. Augmented theories of democracy, on the other hand, might be able to offer slightly better reasons for endorsing democracy (at least here we might hold out hope for passably good political decisions being made), but they require us to rely on and defer to the judgment of political elites in a way that is suspect on empirical grounds.

The second important result I hope to have generated concerns theories of democracy that place substantial burdens on the judgment of citizens (this includes not only epistemic and modified procedural theories but also what, in chapter 4, I called impure deliberative and fairness theories). Given the analysis of framing developed here, I hope to have shown that any theory of democracy that counts epistemic value among the proposed benefits of democratic government ought to be concerned with the effects of framing. More than that, however, I hope that it is clear that such theories need not only worry about framing; they ought to do something about it as well. As chapter 5 is intended to demonstrate, there are things that we can do to help reduce, counteract, and eliminate the effects of framing. To the extent that individual theories of democracy make demands on the judgment of citizens, they ought to be willing to dedicate resources to securing the quality of that judgment. Whether it be by ensuring a wide diversity of frames for political issues, by insulating democratic outcomes from flawed decision making, or by educating citizens so that they avoid falling prey to frames, theories of democracy that rely on the judgment of citizens must ensure that conditions are in place such that we can reasonably expect the political judgment of citizens to be as reliable as they require. Failing to do so, even in the face of mounting empirical evidence regarding framing effects, demonstrates a failure to understand the implications of incorporating epistemic claims into a theory of democracy.[1]

This, it should be noted, provides only a preliminary argument in favor of behavioral democratic theory. If the arguments in the previous chapters are successful, then there is reason to believe that we can learn a good deal more from a broader application of the behavioral approach to democratic theory. By reforming the operative model of human decision making in normative democratic theory to better reflect current scientific understandings of the peculiarities of our perceptions of risk (e.g., base rate neglect[2]), pathologies afflicting group deliberations (e.g., group polarization[3]), and our tendency to overestimate the accuracy of our judgments (e.g., optimism bias[4]), we should be able to come to an even more sophisticated understanding of the relationship between the moral ends of democracy and the proper shape of democratic institutions.

It is my opinion that there is currently too great a disconnect between theorizing about democracy and contemporary political concerns about

[1] In this respect, Robert Talisse's work is a refreshing departure from most normative theories of democracy. Dialogical democracy clearly acknowledges the importance of good judgment in politics and directly addresses the institutional mechanisms necessary for democracy's proper function (see Talisse 2009a, chap. 5 and 2009b). I hope that this represents a new trend in philosophical theories of democracy.

[2] Here, Kahneman and Tversky's research on the representativeness heuristic is a good place to start (Kahneman, Slovic, and Tversky 1982, pt. 2).

[3] Sunstein's recent book *Going to Extremes* (2009a) provides a useful overview of the relevant empirical literature here.

[4] Also referred to as overconfidence bias, there is a large and growing literature on how undue optimism might compromise human decision making. For accessible introductions to this literature and its political importance, see Trout (2005, 2009).

democratic government. Questions about the use of plebiscites and referendums, about low voter turnout and political apathy, about election regulations and funding, and about the design of institutions of review and oversight all seem very distant from most theories of democracy. Although I do not think that democratic theory should be expected to answer all such questions (they are better addressed by policymakers), I do think that democratic theory should speak, at least indirectly, to many of our practical concerns about democratic institutions. One of my aims in developing a behavioral approach to democratic theory is to lessen the gap that currently exists between philosophical theories of democracy and practical problems regarding the design of institutions in democratic societies. I believe that a broader application of the behavioral approach developed here—one that is not limited to an evaluation of framing effects—can help to achieve this goal.

If, by relying on a more realistic picture of human decision making, we can come to a better understanding of the feasibility of different theories of democracy, then democratic theory should be able to speak to practical political questions in a way that is currently not possible. Having a clearer idea of what we can actually expect from democracy and of the costs associated with these expectations should help us to better design institutions and policies capable of meeting those expectations. Behavioral democratic theory can in this way provide us with a clearer understanding of the institutional implications of various theories of democracy.

I should acknowledge that the behavioral approach cannot be expected to settle many long-standing philosophical disagreements within democratic theory. Even a fully worked-out behavioral model of human decision making will not suffice to determine whether we ought to endorse, for example, a purely procedural or an epistemic theory of democracy. It is my hope, however, that once we have fully articulated the costs and benefits associated with various theories of democracy, it will be possible to connect our philosophical disagreements about democratic theory more directly to pressing practical debates about democratic institutions.

References

Amar, A. R. (1984), "Choosing Representatives by Lottery Voting," *Yale Law Journal* 93(7): 1283–1308.

—— (1995), "Lottery Voting: A Thought Experiment," *University of Chicago Legal Forum* 1995 (Voting Rights and Elections): 193–204.

Ariely, D. (2009), *Predictably Irrational: The Hidden Forces That Shape Our Decisions*, New York: Harper.

Ariely, D., J. Huber, and K. Wertenbroch (2005), "When Do Losses Loom Larger Than Gains?," *Journal of Marketing Research* 42(2): 134–138.

Armour, D., and S. E. Taylor (2002), "When Predictions Fail: The Dilemma of Unrealistic Optimism," in *Heuristics and Biases: The Psychology of Intuitive Judgment*, ed. T. Gilovich, D. Griffin, and D. Kahneman, New York: Cambridge University Press.

Armstrong, K., J. S. Schwartz, G. Fitzgerald, M. Putt, and P. A. Ubel (2002), "Effect of Framing as Gain versus Loss on Understanding and Hypothetical Treatment Choices: Survival and Mortality Curves," *Medical Decision Making* 22(1): 76–83.

Arrow, K. J. (1950), "A Difficulty in the Concept of Social Welfare," *Journal of Political Economy* 58(4): 328–346.

—— (1951), *Social Choice and Individual Values*, New York: Wiley.

—— (1982), "Risk Perception in Psychology and Economics," *Economic Inquiry* 20(1): 1–9.

Artz, L., and Y. R. Kamalipour, eds. (2005). *Bring 'Em On: Media and Politics in the Iraq War*, Lanham, MD: Rowman & Littlefield.

Babcock, L., G. Lowenstein, and S. Issacharoff (1997), "Creating Convergence: Debiasing Biased Litigants," *Law & Social Inquiry* 22(4): 913–925.

Baron, J. (1985), *Rationality and Intelligence*, Cambridge: Cambridge University Press.

—— (1995), "Blind Justice: Fairness to Groups and the Do-No-Harm Principle," *Journal of Behavioral Decision Making* 8(2): 71–83.

—— (1998), *Judgment Misguided: Intuition and Error in Public Decision Making*, New York: Oxford University Press.

—— (2001), *Morality and Rational Choice*, Norwell, MA: Springer.

—— (2005), *Rationality and Intelligence*, Cambridge: Cambridge University Press.

—— (2008), *Thinking and Deciding*, 4th ed., New York: Cambridge University Press.

Baron, J., and R. V. Brown, eds. (1991), *Teaching Decision Making to Adolescents*, Hillsdale, NJ: Lawrence Erlbaum Associates.

Barry, B. M. (1965), *Political Argument*, New York: Humanities Press.

Bartels, L. M. (2003a), "Democracy with Attitudes," in *Electoral Democracy*, ed. M. MacKuen and G. Rabinowitz, Ann Arbor: University of Michigan Press.

—— (2003b), "Is 'Popular Rule' Possible? Polls, Political Psychology, and Democracy," *Brookings Review* 21(3): 12–15.

Bateman, C. R., J. P. Fraedrich, and R. Iyer (2002), "Framing Effects within the Ethical Decision Making Process of Consumers," *Journal of Business Ethics* 36(1–2): 119–140.

Baxter, H. W. (2011), *Habermas: The Discourse Theory of Law and Democracy*, Stanford, CA: Stanford University Press.

Bayes, T. (1764), "An Essay toward Solving a Problem in the Doctrine of Chances," *Philosophical Transactions of the Royal Society of London* 53: 370–418.

Bazerman, M. H., J. Baron, and K. Shonk (2001), *You Can't Enlarge the Pie: Six Barriers to Effective Government*, New York: Basic Books.

Becker, G. S. (1976), *The Economic Approach to Human Behavior*, Chicago: University of Chicago Press.

Belsky, G., and T. Gilovich (2010), *Why Smart People Make Big Money Mistakes and How to Correct Them: Lessons from the Life-Changing Science of Behavioral Economics*, New York: Simon & Schuster.

Benhabib, S. (1996), "Toward a Deliberative Model of Democratic Legitimacy," chap. 4 in *Democracy and Difference*, Princeton, NJ: Princeton University Press.

Berg, N., and G. Gigerenzer (2010), "As-If Behavioral Economics: Neoclassical Economics in Disguise?," *History of Economic Ideas* 18(1), 133–166.

Berg, S. (1993a), "Condorcet's Jury Theorem, Dependency among Jurors," *Social Choice and Welfare* 10(1): 87–95.

——— (1993b), "Condorcet's Jury Theorem Revisited," *European Journal of Political Economy* 9(3): 437–446.

——— (1996), "Condorcet's Jury Theorem and the Reliability of Majority Voting," *Group Decision and Negotiation* 5(3): 229–238.

Berinsky, A. J., and D. R. Kinder (2006), "Making Sense of Issues through Media Frames: Understanding the Kosovo Crisis," *Journal of Politics* 68(3): 640–656.

Bernartzi, S., and R. H. Thaler (1995), "Myopic Loss Aversion and the Equity Premium Puzzle," *Quarterly Journal of Economics* 110(1): 73–92.

——— (2002), "How Much Is Investor Autonomy Worth?," *Journal of Finance* 57(4): 1593–1616.

——— (2004), "Save More Tomorrow: Using Behavioral Economics to Increase Employee Saving," *Journal of Political Economy* 112(11): 164–187.

Bernstein, L. M., G. B. Chapman, and A. S. Elstein (1999), "Framing Effects in Choices between Multioutcome Life-Expectancy Lotteries," *Medical Decision Making* 19(3): 324–338.

Besson, S., and J. L. Martí, eds. (2006), *Deliberative Democracy and Its Discontents*, Aldershot, UK: Ashgate.

Beyth-Marom, R., and S. Dekel (1983), "A Curriculum to Improve Thinking under Uncertainty," *Instructional Science* 12: 67–82.

Bishop, M. A., and J. D. Trout (2005), *Epistemology and the Psychology of Human Judgment*, New York: Oxford University Press.

Black, D. (1958), *The Theory of Committees and Elections*, Cambridge: Cambridge University Press.

Black, O. (2005), *Conceptual Foundations of Antitrust*, Cambridge: Cambridge University Press.

Blais, A.-R., and E. U. Weber (2001), "Domain-Specificity and Gender Differences in Decision Making," *Risk, Decision and Policy* 6(1): 47–69.

Bohman, J., and W. Rehg, eds. (1997), *Deliberative Democracy: Essays on Reason and Politics*, Cambridge, MA: MIT Press.

BonJour, L., and E. Sosa (2003), *Epistemic Justification: Internalism vs. Externalism, Foundations vs. Virtues*, Oxford: Blackwell.

Bovens, L., and W. Rabinowicz (2004), "Voting Procedures for Complex Collective Decisions: An Epistemic Perspective," *Ratio Juris* 17(2): 241–258.

Brennan, G. (1989), "Politics with Romance: Towards a Theory of Democratic Socialism," in *The Good Polity: Normative Analysis of the State*, ed. A. P. Hamlin and P. Pettit, Oxford: Blackwell.

Brennan, G., and A. P. Hamlin (2000), *Democratic Devices and Desires*, Cambridge: Cambridge University Press.

——— (2002), "Expressive Constitutionalism," *Constitutional Political Economy* 13(4): 299–311.

Brennan, G., and L. E. Lomasky, eds. (1989), *Politics and Process: New Essays in Democratic Thought*, Cambridge: Cambridge University Press.

——— (1993), *Democracy and Decision: The Pure Theory of Electoral Preference*, Cambridge: Cambridge University Press.

——— (2000), "Is There a Duty to Vote?," *Social Philosophy and Policy* 17: 62–86.

Brennan, G., and P. Pettit (1990), "Unveiling the Vote," *British Journal of Political Science* 20(3): 311–333.

——— (1993), "Hands Invisible and Intangible," *Synthese* 94(2): 191–225.

——— (2002), "Power Corrupts, but Can Office Ennoble?," *Kyklos* 55(2): 157–178.

——— (2004), *The Economy of Esteem: An Essay on Civil and Political Society*, New York: Oxford University Press.

Brennan, J. (2011), *The Ethics of Voting*, Princeton, NJ: Princeton University Press.

Brewer, P. W. (2002), "Framing, Value Words, and Citizens' Explanations of Their Issue Opinions," *Political Communication* 19(3): 303–316.

——— (2007), *Value War: Public Opinion and the Politics of Gay Rights*, Lanham, MD: Rowman & Littlefield.

Brewer, P. W., and K. Gross (2005), "Values, Framing, and Citizens' Thoughts about Policy Issues: Effects on Content and Quantity," *Political Psychology* 26(6): 929–948.

Breyer, S. G. (1993), *Breaking the Vicious Circle: Toward Effective Risk Regulation*, Cambridge, MA: Harvard University Press.

Brock, D., and A. Buchanan (1986), "Deciding for Others," *Milbank Quarterly* 64(Supplement 2): 17–94.

Buchanan, A. E., and D. W. Brock (1989), *Deciding for Others: The Ethics of Surrogate Decisionmaking*, Cambridge: Cambridge University Press.

Buchanan, J. M. (1954), "Social Choice, Democracy and Free Markets," *Journal of Political Economy* 62: 114–123.

Buchanan, J. M., and G. Tullock (1962), *The Calculus of Consent: Logical Foundations of Constitutional Democracy*, Ann Arbor: University of Michigan Press.

Cacioppo, J. T., and R. E. Petty (1982), "The Need for Cognition," *Journal of Personality and Social Psychology* 42(1): 116–131.

Camerer, C. F. (1995), "Individual Decision Making," in *The Handbook of Experimental Economics*, ed. J. H. Kagel and A. E. Roth, Princeton, NJ: Princeton University Press.

——— (1999), "Behavioral Economics: Reunifying Psychology and Economics," *Proceedings of the National Academy of Sciences* 96(19): 10,575–10,577.

——— (2000), "Prospect Theory in the Wild: Evidence from the Field," in *Choices, Values, and Frames*, ed. D. Kahneman and A. Tversky, New York: Cambridge University Press.

——— (2003), *Behavioral Game Theory: Experiments in Strategic Interaction*, Princeton, NJ: Princeton University Press.

——— (2005), "Three Cheers—Psychological, Theoretical, Empirical—for Loss Aversion," *Journal of Marketing Research* 52(2): 129–133.

Camerer, C. F., L. Babcock, G. Lowenstein, and R. H. Thaler (2000), "Labor Supply of New York City Cab Drivers: One Day at a Time," in *Choices, Values, and Frames*, ed. D. Kahneman and A. Tversky, New York: Cambridge University Press.

Camerer, C. F., S. Issacharoff, G. Loewenstein, T. O'Donoghue, and M. Rabin (2003), "Regulation for Conservatives: Behavioral Economics and the Case for 'Asymmetric Paternalism,'" *University of Pennsylvania Law Review* 151: 1211–1254.

Camerer, C. F., G. Loewenstein, and M. Rabin (2003), *Advances in Behavioral Economics*, Princeton, NJ: Princeton University Press.

Caplan, B. (2002), "Sociotropes, Systematic Bias, and Political Failure: Reflections on the Survey of Americans and Economists on the Economy," *Social Science Quarterly* 83(2): 416–435.

——— (2008), *The Myth of the Rational Voter: Why Democracies Choose Bad Policies*, Princeton, NJ: Princeton University Press.

Chapman, G. B., and F. A. Sonnenberg (2000), *Decision Making in Health Care: Theory, Psychology, and Applications*, Cambridge: Cambridge University Press.

Choi, J., J. Laibson, B. Madrian, and A. Metrick (2002), "Defined Contribution Pensions: Plan Rules, Participant Decisions and the Path of Least Resistance," in *Tax Policy and the Economy*, vol. 16, ed. J. M. Poterba, Cambridge, MA: MIT Press.

Chong, D. (1993), "How People Think, Reason and Feel about Rights and Liberties," *American Journal of Political Science* 37: 867–899.

Christensen-Szalanski, J. J. J., and C. F. Willham (1991), "The Hindsight Bias: A Meta-Analysis," *Organizational Behavior and Human Decision Processes* 48: 147–168.

Christiano, T. (2008), *The Constitution of Equality: Democratic Authority and Its Limits*, New York: Oxford University Press.

Clawson, R. A., and E. N. Waltenburg (2003), "Support for a Supreme Court Affirmative Action Decision: A Story in Black and White," *American Politics Research* 31(3): 251–279.

Cobb, M. D. (2005), "Framing Effects on Public Opinion about Nanotechnology," *Science Communication* 27(2): 221–239.

Cohen, D., and J. L. Knetsch (2000), "Judicial Choice and Disparities between Measures of Economic Values," in *Choices, Values, and Frames*, ed. D. Kahneman and A. Tversky, New York: Cambridge University Press.

Cohen, G. A. (2003), "Facts and Principles," *Philosophy & Public Affairs* 31(3): 211–245.

—— (2008), *Rescuing Justice and Equality*, Cambridge, MA: Harvard University Press.

Cohen, J. (1986), "An Epistemic Conception of Democracy," *Ethics* 97(1): 26–38.

—— (1997), "Procedure and Substance in Deliberative Democracy," in *Deliberative Democracy: Essays on Reason and Politics*, ed. J. Bohman and W. Rehg, Cambridge, MA: MIT Press.

—— (2002), "Deliberation and Democratic Legitimacy," in *Democracy*, ed. D. Estlund, Oxford: Blackwell.

—— (2011), "Democracy v. Citizens United?," 2011 Dewey Lecture in Law and Philosophy, University of Chicago Law School, April 20; http://www.law.uchicago.edu/video/cohen042011.

Cohen, J., and J. Rogers (1983), *On Democracy*, New York: Penguin Books.

Coleman, J., and J. Ferejohn (1986), "Democracy and Social Choice," *Ethics* 97(1): 6–25.

Condorcet, M.J.A.N.C. (1976), *Condorcet: Selected Writings*, Indianapolis, IN: Bobbs-Merrill.

Congleton, R. D. (2004), "The Median Voter Model," in *The Encyclopedia of Public Choice*, vol. 2, ed. C. K. Rowley and F. Schneider, New York: Kluwer Academic Press.

Converse, P. E. (1964), "The Nature of Belief Systems in Mass Publics," in *Ideology and Discontent*, ed. D. Apter, New York: Free Press.

—— (1970), "Attitudes and Non-Attitudes: Continuation of a Dialogue," in *The Quantitative Analysis of Social Problems*, ed. E. R. Tufte, Reading, MA: Addison-Wesley.

Converse, P. E., A. Campbell, W. E. Miller, and D. E. Stokes (1964), *The American Voter*, New York: Wiley.

Copp, D. (1995), "Could Political Truth Be a Hazard for Democracy?," in *The Idea of Democracy*, ed. D. Copp, J. Hampton, and J. E. Roemer, Cambridge: Cambridge University Press.

Corrado, A., T. E. Mann, D. R. Ortiz, and T. Potter (2005), *The New Campaign Finance Sourcebook*, Washington, DC: Brookings Institution Press.

Cronqvist, H., and R. H. Thaler (2004), "Design Choices in Privatized Social-Security Systems: Learning from the Swedish Experience," *American Economic Review* 94(2): 424–428.

Dahl, R. A. (1971), *Polyarchy: Participation and Opposition*, New Haven, CT: Yale University Press.

Dalton, R. J. (2006), *Citizen Politics: Public Opinion and Political Parties in Advanced Industrial Democracies*, Washington, DC: CQ Press.

Delli Carpini, M. X. (2004), "Mediating Democratic Engagement: The Impact of Communications on Citizens' Involvement in Political and Civic Life," in *Handbook of Political Communication Research*, ed. L. L. Kaid, Mahwah, NJ: Lawrence Erlbaum Associates.

—— (2005), "News from Somewhere: Journalistic Frames and the Debate over 'Public Journalism,'" in *Framing American Politics*, ed. K. Callaghan and F. Schnell, Pittsburgh, PA: University of Pittsburgh Press.

Delli Carpini, M. X., and S. Keeter (1996), *What Americans Know about Politics and Why It Matters*, New Haven, CT: Yale University Press.

De Martino, B., D. Kumaran, B. Seymour, and R. J. Dolan (2006), "Frames, Biases, and Rational Decision-Making in the Human Brain," *Science* 313(5787): 684–687.

Doris, J. M. (2002), *Lack of Character: Personality and Moral Behavior*, Cambridge: Cambridge University Press.

Downs, A. (1957), *An Economic Theory of Democracy*, New York: Harper.

Druckman, J. N. (2001a), "Evaluating Framing Effects," *Journal of Economic Psychology* 22(1): 91–101.

——— (2001b), "The Implications of Framing Effects for Citizen Competence," *Political Behavior* 23(3): 225–256.

——— (2001c), "On the Limits of Framing Effects: Who Can Frame?," *Journal of Politics* 63(4): 1041–1066.

——— (2004), "Political Preference Formation: Competition, Deliberation, and the (Ir)Relevance of Framing Effects," *American Political Science Review* 98: 671–686.

Druckman, J., and D. Chong (2007), "Framing Public Opinion in Competitive Democracies," *American Political Science Review* 101: 637–655.

——— (2011), "Public-Elite Interactions: Puzzles in Search of Researchers," in *The Oxford Handbook of American Public Opinion and the Media*, ed. R. Y. Shapiro and L. R. Jacobs, New York: Oxford University Press.

Druckman, J. N., C. L. Hennessy, K. St. Charles, and J. Weber (2010), "Competing Rhetoric over Time: Frames versus Cues," *Journal of Politics* 72: 136–148.

Druckman, J. N., and R. McDermott (2008), "Emotion and the Framing of Risky Choice," *Political Behavior* 30(3): 297–321.

Druckman, J. N., and K. R. Nelson (2003), "Framing and Deliberation: How Citizens' Conversations Limit Elite Influence," *American Journal of Political Science* 47(4): 729–745.

Dryzek, J. S. (2000), *Deliberative Democracy and Beyond: Liberals, Critics, Contestations*, New York: Oxford University Press.

——— (2001), "Legitimacy and Economy in Deliberative Democracy," *Political Theory* 29(5): 651–669.

Dryzek, J. S., and C. List (2003), "Social Choice Theory and Deliberative Democracy: A Reconciliation," *British Journal of Political Science* 33(1): 1–28.

Duchon, D., K. J. Dunegan, and S. L. Barton (1989), "Framing the Problem and Making Decisions: The Facts Are Not Enough," *Engineering Management* 36(1): 25–27.

Duverger, M. (1972), "Factors in a Two-Party and Multiparty System," chapter in part 1 of *Party Politics and Pressure Groups: A Comparative Introduction*, New York: Crowell.

Duxbury, N. (1999), *Random Justice: On Lotteries and Legal Decision-Making*, Oxford: Oxford University Press.

Dworkin, R. (1996), *Freedom's Law: The Moral Reading of the American Constitution*, Cambridge, MA: Harvard University Press.

——— (2006a), *Is Democracy Possible Here? Principles for a New Political Debate*, Princeton, NJ: Princeton University Press.

—— (2006b), *Justice in Robes*, Cambridge, MA: Harvard University Press.

Edwards, A., G. Elwyn, J. Covey, E. Matthews, and R. Pill (2001), "Presenting Risk Information: A Review of the Effects of Framing and Other Manipulations on Patient Outcomes," *Journal of Health Communication* 6(1): 61–82.

Elmore, J. G., and G. Gigerenzer (2005), "Benign Breast Disease: The Risks of Communicating Risk," *New England Journal of Medicine* 353(3): 297–299.

Elster, J. (1983), *Sour Grapes: Studies in the Subversion of Rationality*, Cambridge: Cambridge University Press.

—— (1984), *Ulysses and the Sirens: Studies in Rationality and Irrationality*, Cambridge: Cambridge University Press.

—— (1988), "Taming Chance: Randomization in Individual and Social Decisions," in *Tanner Lectures on Human Values*, vol. 9, ed. G. B. Peterson, Salt Lake City: University of Utah Press.

——, ed. (1998), *Deliberative Democracy*, Cambridge: Cambridge University Press.

—— (2000), *Ulysses Unbound: Studies in Rationality, Precommitment, and Constraints*, Cambridge: Cambridge University Press.

Ely, J. H. (1980), *Democracy and Distrust: A Theory of Judicial Review*, Cambridge, MA: Harvard University Press.

—— (1996), *On Constitutional Ground*, Princeton, NJ: Princeton University Press.

Entman, R. M. (1993), "Framing: Toward Clarification of a Fractured Paradigm," *Journal of Communication* 43(4): 51–58.

—— (2003), *Projections of Power: Framing News, Public Opinion, and U.S. Foreign Policy*, Chicago: University of Chicago Press.

Estlund, D. M. (1990), "Democracy without Preference," *Philosophical Review* 99(3): 397–423.

—— (1994), "Opinion Leaders, Independence, and Condorcet's Jury Theorem," *Theory and Decision* 36(2): 131–162.

—— (1995), "Making Truth Safe for Democracy," in *The Idea of Democracy*, ed. D. Copp, J. Hampton, and J. E. Roemer, Cambridge: Cambridge University Press.

—— (1997a), "Beyond Fairness and Deliberation: The Epistemic Dimension of Democratic Authority," in *Deliberative Democracy: Essays on Reason and Politics*, ed. J. Bohman and W. Rehg, Cambridge, MA: MIT Press.

—— (1997b), "The Epistemic Dimension of Democratic Authority," *Modern Schoolman* 74(4): 259–276.

—— (1998), "The Insularity of the Reasonable: Why Political Liberalism Must Admit the Truth," *Ethics* 108(2): 252–275.

—— (2000), "Jeremy Waldron on Law and Disagreement," *Philosophical Studies* 99(1): 111–128.

—— (2001a), "Deliberation and Wide Civility: Response to the Discussants," in *The Boundaries of Freedom of Expression and Order in American Democracy*, ed. T. R. Hensley, Kent, OH: Kent State University Press.

—— (2001b), "Deliberation Down and Dirty," in *The Boundaries of Freedom of Expression and Order in American Democracy*, ed. T. R. Hensley, Kent, OH: Kent State University Press.

Estlund, D. M., ed. (2002a). *Democracy*, Oxford: Blackwell.

—— (2002b). "Political Quality," in *Democracy*, ed. D. M. Estlund, Oxford: Blackwell.

—— (2005), "Democracy and the Real Speech Situation," in *Deliberative Democracy and Its Discontents*, ed. S. Besson and J. L. Martí, Aldershot, UK: Ashgate.

—— (2008), *Democratic Authority: A Philosophical Framework*, Princeton, NJ: Princeton University Press.

Estlund, D. M., J. Waldron, B. Grofman, and S. L. Feld (1989), "Democratic Theory and the Public Interest: Condorcet and Rousseau Revisited," *American Political Science Review* 83(4): 1317–1340.

Fairweather, A., and L. T. Zagzebski, eds. (2001), *Virtue Epistemology: Essays on Epistemic Virtue and Responsibility*, New York: Oxford University Press.

Fatas, E., T. Neugebauer, and P. Tamborero (2007), "How Politicians Make Decisions: A Political Choice Experiment," *Journal of Economics* 92(2): 167–196.

Fischhoff, B. (1982), "Debiasing," in *Judgment under Uncertainty: Heuristics and Biases*, ed. D. Kahneman, P. Slovic, and A. Tversky, New York: Cambridge University Press.

—— (2002), "Heuristics and Biases in Application," in *Heuristics and Biases: The Psychology of Intuitive Judgment*, ed. T. Gilovich, D. Griffin, and D. Kahneman, New York: Cambridge University Press.

Fishkin, J. S. (1991), *Democracy and Deliberation: New Directions for Democratic Reform*, Yale University Press.

Fishkin, J. S., and P. Laslett (2003), *Debating Deliberative Democracy*, Oxford: Blackwell.

Fletcher, G.J.O. (1994), "Assessing Error in Social Judgment," *Psycoloquy* 5(10).

Freedman, P. (2000), "The Political Logic of Framing" (unpublished manuscript).

Freeman, S. (2000), "Deliberative Democracy: A Sympathetic Comment," *Philosophy and Public Affairs* 29(4).

Frisch, D. (1993), "Reasons for Framing Effects," *Organizational Behavior and Human Decision Processes* 54(3): 399–429.

Fuller, L. L. (1978), "The Forms and Limits of Adjudication," *Harvard Law Review* 92(2): 353–409.

Gamliel, E., and E. Peer (2006), "Positive versus Negative Framing Affects Justice Judgments," *Social Justice Research* 19(3): 307–322.

Gamson, W. A. (1992), *Talking Politics*, Cambridge: Cambridge University Press.

Gamson, W. A., and A. Modigliani (1987), "The Changing Culture of Affirmative Action," in *Research in Political Sociology*, vol. 3, ed. R. D. Braungart, Greenwich, CT: JAI Press.

—— (1989), "Media Discourse and Public Opinion on Nuclear Power: A Constructionist Approach," *American Journal of Sociology*, 95(1): 1–37.

Gaus, G. F. (1997a), "Does Democracy Reveal the Voice of the People? Four Takes on Rousseau," *Australasian Journal of Philosophy* 75(2): 141–162.

—— (1997b), "Looking for the Best and Finding None Better: The Epistemic Case for Democracy," *Modern Schoolman* 74(4): 277–284.

Gigerenzer, G. (1991), "How to Make Cognitive Illusions Disappear: Beyond Heuristics and Biases," in *European Review of Social Psychology*, vol. 2, ed. W. Stroebe and M. Hewstone, Chichester, UK: Wiley.

———— (2000), *Adaptive Thinking: Rationality in the Real World*, New York: Oxford University Press.

———— (2005), "I Think, Therefore I Err," *Social Research* 72(1): 195–218.

———— (2007), *Gut Feelings: The Intelligence of the Unconscious*, New York: Viking.

———— (2008), *Rationality for Mortals: How People Cope with Uncertainty*, New York: Oxford University Press.

Gigerenzer, G., and C. Engel, eds. (2006). *Heuristics and the Law*, Cambridge, MA: MIT Press.

Gigerenzer, G., and R. Selten, eds. (2001), *Bounded Rationality: The Adaptive Toolbox*, Cambridge, MA: MIT Press.

Gigerenzer, G., P. M. Todd, and ABC Research Group, eds. (1999), *Simple Heuristics That Make Us Smart*, New York: Oxford University Press.

Gilovich, T. (1991), *How We Know What Isn't So: The Fallibility of Human Reason in Everyday Life*, New York: Free Press.

Gilovich, T., D. W. Griffin, and D. Kahneman, eds. (2002), *Heuristics and Biases: The Psychology of Intuitive Judgment*, New York: Cambridge University Press.

Gintis, H. (2004), "Towards the Unity of the Human Behavioral Sciences," *Politics, Philosophy and Economics* 3(1): 37–57.

Glaeser, E. L. (2006), "Paternalism and Psychology," *Regulation* 29(2): 32–38.

Gold, N., and C. List (2004), "Framing as Path-Dependence," *Economics and Philosophy* 20(2): 253–277.

Goodie, A. S., and E. Fantino (1996), "Learning to Commit or Avoid the Base-Rate Error," *Nature* 380(6571): 247–249.

Goodin, R. E. (2003), *Reflective Democracy*, New York: Oxford University Press.

Goodin, R. E., and D. M. Estlund (2004), "The Persuasiveness of Democratic Majorities," *Politics, Philosophy and Economics* 3(2): 131–142.

Goodwin, B. (2005), *Justice by Lottery*, Exeter, UK: Imprint Academic.

Griffin, D., and A. Tversky (2002), "The Weighing of Evidence and the Determinants of Choice," in *Heuristics and Biases: The Psychology of Intuitive Judgment*, ed. T. Gilovich, D. Griffin, and D. Kahneman, New York: Cambridge University Press.

Grofman, B. (1978), "Judgmental Competence of Individuals and Groups in a Dichotomous Choice Situation: Is a Majority of Heads Better Than One?," *Journal of Mathematical Sociology* 6: 47–60.

Grofman, B., and S. L. Feld (1988), "Rousseau's General Will: A Condorcetian Perspective," *American Political Science Review* 82(2): 567–576.

Gulati, G. M., J. J. Rachlinski, and D. C. Langevoort (2004), "Fraud by Hindsight," *Northwestern University Law Review* 98: 773–825.

Guthrie, C., J. J. Rachlinski, and A. J. Wistrich (2001), "Inside the Judicial Mind," *Cornell Law Review* 86(4): 777–830.

———— (2002), "Judging by Heuristic: Cognitive Illusions in Judicial Decision Making," *Judicature* 86(1): 44–50.

———— (2005), "Can Judges Ignore Inadmissible Information? The Difficulty of Deliberately Disregarding," *University of Pennsylvania Law Review* 153(4): 1251–1345.

Gutmann, A., and D. F. Thompson (1996), *Democracy and Disagreement*, Cambridge, MA: Harvard University Press.

Habermas, J. (1996), *Between Facts and Norms: Contributions to a Discourse Theory of Law and Democracy*, Cambridge, MA: MIT Press.

—— (2005), "Concluding Comments on Empirical Approaches to Deliberative Politics," *Acta Politica* 40(3): 384–392.

—— (2006), "Political Communication in Media Society: Does Democracy Still Enjoy an Epistemic Dimension? The Impact of Normative Theory on Empirical Research," *Communication Theory* 16(4): 411–426.

Habermas, J., C. Cronin, and P. De Greiff (1998), *The Inclusion of the Other: Studies in Political Theory*, Cambridge, MA: MIT Press.

Hancock, A.-M. (2004), *The Politics of Disgust: The Public Identity of the Welfare Queen*, New York: New York University Press.

Hardin, R. (1999a), *Liberalism, Constitutionalism, and Democracy*, New York: Oxford University Press.

—— (1999b), "Public Choice versus Democracy," in *The Idea of Democracy*, ed. D. Copp, J. Hampton, and J. E. Roemer, Cambridge: Cambridge University Press.

—— (2009), *How Do You Know? The Economics of Ordinary Knowledge*, Princeton, NJ: Princeton University Press.

Hart, H. M., A. M. Sacks, W. N. Eskridge, and P. P. Frickey (1994), *The Legal Process: Basic Problems in the Making and Application of Law*, New York: Foundation Press.

Hasseldine, J., and P. A. Hite (2003), "Framing, Gender and Tax Compliance," *Journal of Economic Psychology* 24(4): 517–533.

Hastie, R., S. Penrod, and N. Pennington (2002), *Inside the Jury*, Clark, NJ: Lawbook Exchange.

Hersch, J., and W. K. Viscusi (2004), "Punitive Damages: How Judges and Juries Perform," *Journal of Legal Studies* 33(1): 1–36.

Highhouse, S., and K. Bottrill (1995), "The Influence of Social (Mis)Information on Memory for Behavior in an Employment Interview," *Organizational Behavior and Human Decision Processes* 62: 220–229.

Hintikka, J. (2004), "A Fallacious Fallacy?," *Synthese* 140: 25–35.

Hiscox, M. J. (2006), "Through a Glass and Darkly: Attitudes toward International Trade and the Curious Effects of Issue Framing," *International Organization* 60(3): 755–780.

Hurd, S. D., D. C. Langevoort, J. J. Rachlinski, F. Jourden, R. Korobkin, C. Jolls, R. K. Rasmussen, E. L. Rubin, S. Issacharoff, T.S. Ulen, and J. Arlen, (1998), "Symposium: The Legal Implications of Psychology: Human Behavior, Behavioral Economics, and the Law," *Vanderbilt Law Review* 51: 1495–1788.

Hyman, H. H., and P. B. Sheatsley (1950), "The Current Status of American Public Opinion," in *The Teaching of Contemporary Affairs*, ed. J. C. Payne, Washington, DC: National Council of Social Studies.

Iyengar, S. (1990), "Framing Responsibility for Political Issues: The Case of Poverty," *Political Behavior* 12(1): 19–40.

Johnson, E. J., and D. Goldstein (2003), "Do Defaults Save Lives?," *Science* 302(5649): 1338–1339.

Johnson, E. J., J. Hershey, J. Mezaros, and H. Kunreuther (2000), "Framing, Probability Distortions, and Insurance Decisions," in *Choices, Values, and Frames*, ed. D. Kahneman and A. Tversky, New York: Cambridge University Press.

Jolls, C. (2006), "Behavioral Law and Economics," in *Economic Institutions and Behavioral Economics*, ed. P. Diamond, Princeton, NJ: Princeton University Press.

Jolls, C., and C. R. Sunstein (2006), "Debiasing through Law," *Journal of Legal Studies* 35: 199–242.

Jolls, C., C. R. Sunstein, and R. H. Thaler (1998), "A Behavioral Approach to Law and Economics," *Stanford Law Review* 50(5): 1471–1550.

Joslyn, M. R., and D. P. Haider-Markel (2002), "Framing Effects on Personal Opinion and Perception of Public Opinion: The Cases of Physician-Assisted Suicide and Social Security," *Social Science Quarterly* 83(3): 690–707.

Kahneman, D. (2000), "Experienced Utility and Objective Happiness: A Moment-Based Approach," in *Choices, Values, and Frames*, ed. D. Kahneman and A. Tversky, New York: Cambridge University Press.

—— (2002), "Maps of Bounded Rationality: A Perspective on Intuitive Judgment and Choice," Nobel Prize lecture; http://www.nobelprize.org/nobel_prizes/economics/laureates/2002/kahnemann-lecture.pdf.

—— (2003), "Maps of Bounded Rationality: Psychology for Behavioral Economics," *American Economic Review* 93(5): 1449–1475.

Kahneman, D., J. L. Knetsch, and R. H. Thaler (2000a), "Anomalies: The Endowment Effect, Loss Aversion and Status Quo Bias," in *Choices, Values, and Frames*, ed. D. Kahneman and A. Tversky, New York: Cambridge University Press.

—— (2000b), "Fairness as a Constraint on Profit Seeking: Entitlements in the Market," in *Choices, Values, and Frames*, ed. D. Kahneman and A. Tversky, New York: Cambridge University Press.

Kahneman, D., and D. Lovallo (2000), "Timid Choices and Bold Forecasts: A Cognitive Perspective on Risk Taking," in *Choices, Values, and Frames*, ed. D. Kahneman and A. Tversky, New York: Cambridge University Press.

Kahneman, D., I. Ritov, and D. Schkade (2000), "Economic Preferences or Attitude Expressions? An Analysis of Dollar Responses to Public Issues," in *Choices, Values, and Frames*, ed. D. Kahneman and A. Tversky, New York: Cambridge University Press.

Kahneman, D., P. Slovic, and A. Tversky, eds. (1982), *Judgment under Uncertainty: Heuristics and Biases*, New York: Cambridge University Press.

Kahneman, D., and A. Tversky (1981), "The Framing of Decisions and the Psychology of Choice," *Science* 211(4481): 453–458.

—— (1986), "Rational Choice and the Framing of Decisions," *Journal of Business* 59(4): S251–S278.

—— (2000a), "Advances in Prospect Theory: Cumulative Representation of Uncertainty," in *Choices, Values, and Frames*, ed. D. Kahneman and A. Tversky, New York: Cambridge University Press.

—— (2000b), "Choices, Values, and Frames," in *Choices, Values, and Frames*, ed. D. Kahneman and A. Tversky, New York: Cambridge University Press.

Kahneman, D., and A. Tversky, eds. (2000c), *Choices, Values, and Frames*, New York: Cambridge University Press.

———— (2000d), "Prospect Theory: An Analysis of Decision under Risk," in *Choices, Values, and Frames*, ed. D. Kahneman and A. Tversky, New York: Cambridge University Press.

Kamin, K. A., and J. J. Rachlinski (1995), "Ex Post ≠ Ex Ante: Determining Liability in Hindsight," *Law and Human Behavior* 19(1): 89–104.

Kanazawa, S. (1999), "Using Laboratory Experiments to Test Theories of Corporate Behavior," *Rationality and Society* 11(4): 443–461.

Kang, J., and M. R. Banaji (2006), "Fair Measures: A Behavioral Realist Revision of 'Affirmative Action,'" *California Law Review* 94: 1063–1118.

Kelly, J. T. (forthcoming), "Libertarian Paternalism, Utilitarianism, and Justice," in *Paternalism: Theory and Practice*, ed. C. Coons and M. Weber, Cambridge: Cambridge University Press.

Kelman, M., Y. Rottenstreich, and A. Tversky (1996), "Context-Dependence in Legal Decision-Making," *Journal of Legal Studies* 25(287): 295–297.

Kim, S., D. Goldstein, L. Hasher, and R. T. Zacks (2005), "Framing Effects in Younger and Older Adults," *Journals of Gerontology Series B: Psychological Sciences and Social Sciences* 60: 215–218.

Kinder, D. R., and D. R. Kiewiet (1981), "Sociotropic Politics: The American Case," *British Journal of Political Science* 11(2): 129–161.

Kinder, D. R., and L. M. Sanders (1996), *Divided by Color: Racial Politics and Democratic Ideals*, Chicago: University of Chicago Press.

Kinsey, K. A., H. G. Grasmick, and K. W. Smith (1991), "Framing Justice: Taxpayer Evaluations of Personal Tax Burdens," *Law and Society Review* 25(4): 845–874.

Klein, D. B. (2004a), "Reply to Sunstein," *Econ Journal Watch* 1(2): 274–276.

———— (2004b), "Statist Quo Bias," *Econ Journal Watch* 1(2): 260–271.

Koehler, D. J., L. Brenner, and D. Griffin (2002), "The Calibration of Expert Judgment: Heuristics and Biases beyond the Laboratory," in *Heuristics and Biases: The Psychology of Intuitive Judgment*, ed. T. Gilovich, D. Griffin, and D. Kahneman, New York: Cambridge University Press.

Koehler, J. J. (1993), "The Base Rate Fallacy Myth," *Psycoloquy* 4(49).

Kühberger, A. (1998), "The Influence of Framing on Risky Decisions: A Meta-Analysis," *Organizational Behavior and Human Decision Processes* 75(1): 23–55.

Kühberger, A., M. Schulte-Mecklenbeck, and J. Perner (1999), "The Effects of Framing, Reflection, Probability, and Payoff on Risk Preference in Choice Tasks," *Organizational Behavior and Human Decision Processes* 78(3): 204–231.

Kuran, T., and C. R. Sunstein (1999), "Availability Cascades and Risk Regulation," *Stanford Law Review* 51(4): 683–768.

Lacy, D. (2001a), "Nonseparable Preferences, Measurement Error, and Unstable Survey Responses," *Political Analysis* 9(2): 1–21.

———— (2001b), "A Theory of Nonseparable Preferences in Survey Responses," *American Journal of Political Science* 45(2): 239–258.

Ladha, K. K. (1992), "The Condorcet Jury Theorem, Free Speech, and Correlated Votes," *American Journal of Political Science* 36(3): 617–634.

Lakoff, G. (2004), *Don't Think of an Elephant! Know Your Values and Frame the Debate: The Essential Guide for Progressives*, White River Junction, VT: Chelsea Green Publishing.

———— (2009), *The Political Mind: A Cognitive Scientist's Guide to Your Brain and Its Politics*, New York: Penguin.

LeBoeuf, R. A., and E. Shafir (2003), "Deep Thoughts and Shallow Frames: On the Susceptibility to Framing Effects," *Journal of Behavioral Decision Making* 16(2): 77–92.

Lee, T.-T. (2005), "Media Effects on Political Disengagement Revisited," *Journalism and Mass Communication Quarterly* 82(2): 416–433.

Levi, I. (1985), "Illusions about Uncertainty," *British Journal for the Philosophy of Science* 36: 331–340.

Levin, I. P., and G. J. Gaeth (1988), "How Consumers Are Affected by the Framing of Attribute Information before and after Consuming the Product," *Journal of Consumer Research* 15(3): 374–378.

Levin, I. P., G. J. Gaeth, J. Schreiber, and M. Lauriola (2002), "A New Look at Framing Effects: Distribution of Effect Sizes, Individual Differences, and Independence of Types of Effects," *Organizational Behavior and Human Decision Processes* 88(1): 411–429.

Levin, I. P., S. L. Schneider, and G. J. Gaeth (1998), "All Frames Are Not Created Equal: A Typology and Critical Analysis of Framing Effects," *Organizational Behavior and Human Decision Processes* 76(2): 149–188.

Levine, A. (1976), *The Politics of Autonomy: A Kantian Reading of Rousseau's Social Contract*, Amherst: University of Massachusetts Press.

Levy, J. S. (2000), "Loss Aversion, Framing Effects, and International Conflict: Perspectives from Prospect Theory," in *Handbook of War Studies II*, ed. M. I. Midlarsky, Ann Arbor: University of Michigan Press.

Lewis, M. (2003), *Moneyball: The Art of Winning an Unfair Game*, New York: W. W. Norton.

Lichtenstein, S., and P. Slovic, eds. (2006), *The Construction of Preference*, Cambridge: Cambridge University Press.

Lipkus, I. M., M. Biradavolu, K. Fenn, P. Keller, and B. K. Rimer (2001), "Informing Women about Their Breast Cancer Risks: Truth and Consequences," *Health Communication* 13(2): 206–226.

Lipsey, R. G., and K. Lancaster (1956), "The General Theory of Second Best," *Review of Economic Studies* 24: 11–32.

List, C. (2004), "A Model of Path Dependence in Decisions over Multiple Propositions," *American Political Science Review* 98(3): 495–513.

List, C., and R. E. Goodin (2001), "Epistemic Democracy: Generalizing the Condorcet Jury Theorem," *Journal of Political Philosophy* 9(3): 277–306.

List, C., and P. Pettit (2011), *Group Agency: The Possibility, Design, and Status of Corporate Agents*, Oxford: Oxford University Press.

Loke, W. H., and S. L. L. Lau (1992), "Effects of Framing and Mathematical Experience on Judgments," *Bulletin of the Psychonomic Society* 30(5): 393–395.

Loke, W. H., and K. F. Tan (1992), "Effects of Framing and Missing Information in Expert and Novice Judgment," *Bulletin of the Psychonomic Society* 30(3): 187–190.

Loomes, G., and R. Sugden (1982), "Regret Theory: An Alternative Theory of Rational Choice under Uncertainty," *Economic Journal* 92(368): 805–824.

Lowenstein, G., and D. Adler (2000), "A Bias in the Prediction of Tastes," in *Choices, Values, and Frames*, ed. D. Kahneman and A. Tversky, New York: Cambridge University Press.

Lupia, A. (2002), "Deliberation Disconnected: What It Takes to Improve Civic Competence," *Law and Contemporary Problems* 65(3): 133–150.

Lupia, A., M. D. McCubbins, and S. L. Popkin, eds. (2000), *Elements of Reason: Cognition, Choice, and the Bounds of Rationality*, Cambridge: Cambridge University Press.

Lyons, D. B. (1987), "Substance, Process and Outcome in Constitutional Theory," *Cornell Law Review* 72: 745–764.

––––––– (1993a), "Basic Rights and Constitutional Interpretation," chap. 9 in *Moral Aspects of Legal Theory: Essays on Law, Justice, and Political Responsibility*, Cambridge: Cambridge University Press.

––––––– (1993b), "Constitutional Interpretation and Original Meaning," chap. 7 in *Moral Aspects of Legal Theory: Essays on Law, Justice, and Political Responsibility*, Cambridge: Cambridge University Press.

––––––– (1993c), "A Preface to Constitutional Theory," chap. 8 in *Moral Aspects of Legal Theory: Essays on Law, Justice, and Political Responsibility*, Cambridge: Cambridge University Press.

MacCoun, R. J. (1989), "Experimental Research on Jury Decision–Making," *Science* 244(4908): 1046–1050.

MacLean, D. (2006), "Informed Consent and the Construction of Values," in *The Construction of Preferences*, ed. S. Lichtenstein and P. Slovic, New York: Cambridge University Press.

Madrian, B., and D. Shea (2001), "The Power of Suggestion: Inertia in 401(k) Participation and Savings Behaviour," *Quarterly Journal of Economics* 116(4): 1149–1187.

Magleby, D. B., and A. Corrado (2011), *Financing the 2008 Election*, Washington, DC: Brookings Institution Press.

Marmor, A. (2007), "Are Constitutions Legitimate?," *Canadian Journal of Law and Jurisprudence,* 20(1): 69–112.

Martí, J. L. (2006), "The Epistemic Conception of Deliberative Democracy Defended: Reasons, Rightness and Equal Political Autonomy," in *Deliberative Democracy and Its Discontents*, ed. S. Besson and J. L. Martí, Aldershot, UK: Ashgate.

Mashaw, J. L. (1997), *Greed, Chaos, and Governance: Using Public Choice to Improve Public Law*, New Haven, CT: Yale University Press.

Mayhorn, C. B., A. D. Fisk, and J. D. Whittle (2002), "Decisions, Decisions: Analysis of Age, Cohort, and Time of Testing on Framing of Risky Decision Options," *Human Factors* 44(4): 515–521.

McCaffery, E. J., D. Kahneman, and M. L. Spitzer (2002), "Framing the Jury," in *Behavioral Law and Economics*, ed. C. R. Sunstein, Cambridge: Cambridge University Press.

McFadden, D. (2006), "Free Markets and Fettered Consumers," *American Economic Review* 96(1): 5–29.

McKenzie, C.R.M. (2004), "Framing Effects in Inference Tasks—and Why They Are Normatively Defensible," *Memory & Cognition* 32(6): 874–885.

McNeil, B. J., S. G. Pauker, H. C. Sox, and A. Tversky (1982), "On the Elicitation of Preferences for Alternative Therapies," *New England Journal of Medicine* 306: 1259–1262.

Menand, L. (2005), "Everybody's an Expert: Putting Predictions to the Test," *New Yorker*, December 5.

Meyerowitz, B. E., and S. Chaiken (1987), "The Effect of Message Framing on Breast Self-Examination: Attitudes, Intentions, and Behavior," *Journal of Personality and Social Psychology* 52(3): 500–510.

Miller, N. R. (1996), "Information, Individual Errors, and Collective Performance: Empirical Evidence on the Condorcet Jury Theorem," *Group Decision and Negotiation* 5(3): 211–228.

Mitchell, G. (2002a), "Taking Behavioralism Too Seriously: The Unwarranted Pessimism of the New Behavioral Analysis of Law," *William and Mary Law Review* 43(5): 1907–2022.

—— (2002b), "Why Law and Economics' Perfect Rationality Should Not Be Traded for Behavioral Law and Economics' Equal Incompetence," *Georgetown Law Review* 91: 67–168.

—— (2005), "Libertarian Paternalism Is an Oxymoron," *Northwestern University Law Review* 73: 133–156.

Moxey, A., D. O'Connell, P. McGettigan, and D. Henry (2003), "Describing Treatment Effects to Patients: How They Are Expressed Makes a Difference," *Journal of General Internal Medicine* 18(11): 948–953.

Nash, J. R. (2006), "Framing Effects and Regulatory Choice," *Notre Dame Law Review* 82(7): 313–372.

Neale, M. A., and G. B. Northcraft (1986), "Experts, Amateurs, and Refrigerators: Comparing Expert and Amateur Negotiators in a Novel Task," *Organizational Behavior and Human Decision Processes* 38(3): 305–317.

Nelson, T. E., R. A. Clawson, and Z. M. Oxley (1997), "Media Framing of a Civil Liberties Conflict and Its Effect on Tolerance," *American Political Science Review* 91(3): 567–583.

Nelson, T. E., Z. M. Oxley, and R. A. Clawson (1997), "Toward a Psychology of Framing Effects," *Political Behavior* 19(3): 221–246.

Nincic, M. (1997), "Loss Aversion and the Domestic Context of Military Intervention," *Political Research Quarterly* 50(1): 197–120.

Nino, C. S. (1996), *The Constitution of Deliberative Democracy*, New Haven, CT: Yale University Press.

Novemsky, N., and D. Kahneman (2005a), "The Boundaries of Loss Aversion," *Journal of Marketing Research* 42(2): 119–128.

—— (2005b), "How Do Intentions Affect Loss Aversion?," *Journal of Marketing Research* 42(2): 139–140.

Nussbaum, M. C. (2000), *Women and Human Development: The Capabilities Approach*, Cambridge: Cambridge University Press.

Nussbaum, M. C. (2007), *Frontiers of Justice: Disability, Nationality, Species Membership*, Cambridge, MA: Harvard University Press.

Olsaretti, S., ed. (2006), *Preferences and Well-Being*, Cambridge: Cambridge University Press.

Padovani, C. (2005), *A Fatal Attraction: Public Television and Politics in Italy*, Lanham, MD: Rowman & Littlefield.

Parisi, F., and V. L. Smith (2005), *The Law and Economics of Irrational Behavior*, Stanford, CA: Stanford University Press.

Parry, G. (2008), *Political Elites*, New York: Columbia University Press.

Pateman, C. (1986), "Social Choice or Democracy? A Comment on Coleman and Ferejohn," *Ethics* 97(1): 39–46.

Pennington, N., and R. Hastie (1992), "Examining the Evidence: Tests of the Story Model for Juror Decision Making," *Journal of Personality and Social Psychology* 62(2): 189–206.

Petrinovich, L., and P. O'Neill (1996), "Influence of Wording and Framing Effects on Moral Intuitions," *Ethology and Sociobiology* 17: 145–171.

Piattelli-Palmarini, M. (1994), *Inevitable Illusions: How Mistakes of Reason Rule Our Minds*, New York: Wiley.

Pildes, R. H., and E. S. Anderson (1990), "Slinging Arrows at Democracy: Social Choice Theory, Value Pluralism, and Democratic Politics," *Columbia Law Review* 90(8): 2121–2122.

Popkin, S. L. (1991), *The Reasoning Voter: Communication and Persuasion in Presidential Campaigns*, Chicago: University of Chicago Press.

Posner, R. A. (1998), "Rational Choice, Behavioral Economics, and the Law," *Stanford Law Review* 50(5): 1551–1575.

—— (2003), *Law, Pragmatism, and Democracy*, Cambridge, MA: Harvard University Press.

—— (2004), *Catastrophe: Risk and Response*, New York: Oxford University Press.

Post, T., M. J. van den Assem, G. Baltussen, and R. H. Thaler (2008), "Deal or No Deal? Decision Making under Risk in a Large-Payoff Game Show," *American Economic Review* 98(1): 38–71.

Przeworski, A. (1999), "Minimalist Conception of Democracy: A Defense," in *Democracy's Values*, ed. I. Shapiro and C. Hacker-Cordón, Cambridge: Cambridge University Press.

—— (2003), "Why Do Political Parties Obey Results of Elections?," in *Democracy and the Rule of Law*, ed. A. Przeworski and J. M. Maravall, Cambridge: Cambridge University Press.

Quine, W. V. (1960), *Word and Object*, Cambridge, MA: Technology Press of the Massachusetts Institute of Technology.

Rachlinski, J. J. (2003), "The Uncertain Psychological Case for Paternalism," *Northwestern University Law Review* 97(3): 1165–1225.

—— (2006), "Cognitive Errors, Individual Differences, and Paternalism," *University of Chicago Law Review* 73(1): 207–230.

Raghubir, P., and G. Menon (2001), "Framing Effects in Risk Perceptions of AIDS," *Marketing Letters* 12(2): 145–155.

Rasinski, K. A. (1989), "The Effect of Question Wording on Public Support for Government Spending," *Public Opinion Quarterly* 53(3): 388–394.

Rawls, J. (1993), *Political Liberalism*, New York: Columbia University Press.

——— (1999a), *The Law of Peoples: With "The Idea of Public Reason Revisited,"* Cambridge, MA: Harvard University Press.

——— (1999b), *A Theory of Justice*, Cambridge, MA: Harvard University Press.

Redelmeier, D. A., P. Rozin, and D. Kahneman (1993), "Understanding Patients' Decisions: Cognitive and Emotional Perspectives," *Journal of the American Medical Association* 270(1): 72–76.

Redelmeier, D. A., and E. Shafir (1995), "Medical Decision Making in Situations That Offer Multiple Alternatives," *Journal of the American Medical Association* 273(4): 302–305.

Redelmeier, D. A., and A. Tversky (1990), "Discrepancy between Medical Decisions for Individual Patients and for Groups," *New England Journal of Medicine* 322(16): 1162–1164.

Revesz, R. L. (2008), *Environmental Law and Policy*, New York: Foundation Press.

Riker, W. H. (1982a), *Liberalism against Populism: A Confrontation between the Theory of Democracy and the Theory of Social Choice*, San Francisco: W. H. Freeman.

——— (1982b), "The Two-Party System and Duverger's Law: An Essay on the History of Political Science," *American Political Science Review* 76(4): 753–766.

Robbennolt, J. K. (2002), "Punitive Damage Decision Making: The Decisions of Citizens and Trial Court Judges," *Law and Human Behavior* 26(3): 315–341.

Roberts, M. L., P. A. Hite, and C. F. Bradley (1994), "Understanding Attitudes toward Progressive Taxation," *Public Opinion Quarterly* 58(2): 165–190.

Ronnlund, M., E. Karlsson, E. Laggnas, L. Larsson, and T. Lindstrom (2005), "Risky Decision Making across Three Arenas of Choice: Are Younger and Older Adults Differently Susceptible to Framing Effects?," *Journal of General Psychology* 132(1): 81–92.

Rostain, T. (2000), "Educating Homo Economicus: Cautionary Notes on the New Behavioral Law and Economics Movement," *Law and Society Review* 34(4): 973–1006.

Sanna, L. J., and N. Schwarz (2003), "Debiasing the Hindsight Bias: The Role of Accessibility Experiences and (Mis)Attributions," *Journal of Experimental Social Psychology* 39(3): 287–295.

Sanna, L. J., N. Schwarz, and E. M. Small (2002), "Accessibility Experiences and the Hindsight Bias: I Knew It All Along versus It Could Never Have Happened," *Memory & Cognition* 30(8): 1288–1296.

Sanna, L. J., N. Schwarz, and S. L. Stocker (2002), "When Debiasing Backfires: Accessible Content and Accessibility Experiences in Debiasing Hindsight," *Journal of Experimental Psychology: Learning, Memory, and Cognition* 28(3): 497–502.

Saunders, B. (2010), "Democracy, Political Equality, and Majority Rule," *Ethics* 121(1):148–177.

Schkade, D., C. R. Sunstein, and R. Hastie (2007), "What Happened on Deliberation Day?," *California Law Review* 95(3): 915–940.

Schnell, F., and K. Callaghan (2005), "Terrorism, Media Frames, and Framing Effects: A Macro- and Microlevel Analysis," in *Framing American Politics*, ed. K. Callaghan and F. Schnell, Pittsburgh, PA: University of Pittsburgh Press.

Schuck, A.R.T., and C. H. de Vreese (2006), "Between Risk and Opportunity: News Framing and Its Effects on Public Support for E.U. Enlargement," *European Journal of Communication* 21(1): 5–32.

Schuman, H., G. Kalton, and J. Ludwig (1983), "Context and Contiguity in Survey Questionnaires," *Public Opinion Quarterly* 47(1): 112–115.

Schuman, H., and S. Presser (1981), *Questions and Answers in Attitude Surveys: Experiments on Question Form, Wording, and Context*, New York: Academic Press.

Schumpeter, J. A. (1950), *Capitalism, Socialism, and Democracy*, New York: Harper.

Seburn, M. (2001), "A Meta-Analysis of Structural Differences in Framing Problems," PhD diss., University of Massachusetts.

Sellars, W. (1963), "Philosophy and the Scientific Image of Man," chap. 1 in *Science, Perception and Reality*, Atascadero, CA: Ridgeview.

Sen, A. K. (1970), *Collective Choice and Social Welfare*, San Francisco: Holden-Day.

——— (1999a), *Choice, Welfare, and Measurement*, Cambridge, MA: Harvard University Press.

——— (1999b), "The Possibility of Social Choice," *American Economic Review* 89(3): 349–378.

Sethi-Iyengar, S., G. Huberman, and G. Jiang (2004), "How Much Choice Is Too Much? Contributions to 401(k) Retirement Plans," in *Pension Design and Structure: New Lessons from Behavioral Finance*, ed. O. S. Mitchell and S. P. Utkus, New York: Oxford University Press.

Shafir, E., P. Diamond, and A. Tversky (2000), "Money Illusion," in *Choices, Values, and Frames*, ed. D. Kahneman and A. Tversky, New York: Cambridge University Press.

Shafir, E., and R. A. LeBoeuf (2002), "Rationality," *Annual Review of Psychology* 53(1): 491–517.

Shefrin, H. (2002), *Beyond Greed and Fear: Understanding Behavioral Finance and the Psychology of Investing*, New York: Oxford University Press.

Sher, S., and C.R.M. McKenzie (2006), "Information Leakage from Logically Equivalent Frames," *Cognition* 101(3): 467–494.

Shleifer, A. (2000), *Inefficient Markets: An Introduction to Behavioral Finance*, New York: Oxford University Press.

Shrader-Frechette, K. S. (1995), "Evaluating the Expertise of Experts," *Risk: Environment, Health, and Safety* 6(2): 115–126.

——— (2006), "Laws of Fear: Beyond the Precautionary Principle by Cass Sunstein," *Ethics & International Affairs* 20(1): 123–125.

Sieck, W., and F. J. Yates (1997), "Exposition Effects on Decision Making: Choice and Confidence in Choice," *Organizational Behavior and Human Decision Processes* 70: 207–219.

Simon, A., and M. Xenos (2000), "Media Framing and Effective Public Deliberation," *Political Communication* 17(4): 363–376.

Simon, A. F., N. S. Fagley, and J. G. Halleran (2004), "Decision Framing: Moderating Effects of Individual Differences and Cognitive Processing," *Journal of Behavioral Decision Making* 17(2): 77–93.

Simon, H. A. (1955), "A Behavioral Model of Rational Choice," *Quarterly Journal of Economics* 69: 99–118.

Simonson, I., and A. Tversky (1992), "Choice in Context: Tradeoff Contrast and Extremeness Aversion," *Journal of Marketing Research* 29(3): 281–295.

Sinnott-Armstrong, W. (2008), "Framing Moral Intuitions," in *Moral Psychology*, vol. 2, *The Cognitive Science of Morality*, ed. W. Sinnott-Armstrong. Cambridge, MA: MIT Press.

Skinner, B. F. (1953), *Science and Human Behavior*, New York: Macmillan.

Slovic, P. (2000), "The Construction of Preference," in *Choices, Values, and Frames*, ed. D. Kahneman and A. Tversky, New York: Cambridge University Press.

Smith, A. C., and E. Greene (2005), "Conduct and Its Consequences: Attempts at Debiasing Jury Judgments," *Law and Human Behavior* 29(5): 505–526.

Smith, J. W. (1961), "Impossibility and Morals," *Mind* 70(279): 362–375.

Smith, S. M., and I. P. Levin (1996), "Need for Cognition and Choice Framing Effects," *Journal of Behavioral Decision Making* 9(4): 283–290.

Smith, T. W. (1987), "That Which We Call Welfare by Any Other Name Would Smell Sweeter: An Analysis of the Impact of Question Wording on Response Patterns," *Public Opinion Quarterly* 51(1): 75–83.

Sniderman, P. M. (2000), "Taking Sides," in *Elements of Reason: Cognition, Choice, and the Bounds of Rationality*, ed. A. Lupia, M. D. McCubbins, and S. L. Popkin, Cambridge: Cambridge University Press.

Sniderman, P. M., and M. S. Levendusky (2007), "An Institutional Theory of Political Choice," in *The Oxford Handbook of Political Behavior*, ed. R. J. Dalton and H.-D. Klingemann, New York: Oxford University Press.

Sniderman, P. M., and S. M. Theriault (2004), "The Structure of Political Argument and the Logic of Issue Framing," in *Studies in Public Opinion: Gauging Attitudes, Nonattitudes, Measurement Error and Change*, ed. W. E. Saris and P. M. Sniderman, Princeton, NJ: Princeton University Press.

Somin, I. (2004), "Political Ignorance and the Countermajoritarian Difficulty: A New Perspective on the Central Obsession of Constitutional Theory," *Iowa Law Review* 89(4): 1287–1372.

——— (2010), "Deliberative Democracy and Political Ignorance," *Critical Review* 22(2–3): 253–279.

Stevenson, D. (2005), "Libertarian Paternalism: The Cocaine Vaccine as a Test Case for the Sunstein/Thaler Model," *Rutgers Journal of Law and Urban Policy* 3(1): 4–61.

Stich, S. P., J. M. Doris, and E. Roedder (2010), "Altruism," in *The Moral Psychology Handbook*, ed. J. M. Doris and the Moral Psychology Group, Oxford: Oxford University Press.

Stoddard, J. E., and E. F. Fern (1999), "Risk-Taking Propensity in Supplier Choice: Differences by Sex and Decision Frame in a Simulated Organizational Buying Context," *Psychology and Marketing* 16(7): 563–582.

Sunstein, C. R. (1984), "Naked Preferences and the Constitution," *Columbia Law Review* 84(7): 1689–1732.

——— (1990), "Republicanism and the Preference Problem," *Chicago-Kent Law Review* 66(1): 181–205.

Sunstein, C. R. (1992), "Preferences and Politics," in *Democracy: Theory and Practice*, ed. J. Arthur, Belmont, CA: Wadsworth.

—— (1993a), "Democracy and Shifting Preferences," in *The Idea of Democracy*, ed. D. Copp, J. Hampton, and J. E. Roemer, Cambridge: Cambridge University Press.

—— (1993b), "Endogenous Preferences, Environmental Law," *Journal of Legal Studies* 22(2): 217–254.

—— (1997), "Behavioral Analysis of Law," *University of Chicago Law Review* 64(4): 1175–1195.

—— (1999), *One Case at a Time: Judicial Minimalism on the Supreme Court*, Cambridge, MA: Harvard University Press.

——, ed. (2000a), *Behavioral Law and Economics*, Cambridge: Cambridge University Press.

—— (2000b), "Deliberative Trouble? Why Groups Go to Extremes," *Yale Law Journal* 110(1): 71–119.

—— (2001), *Designing Democracy: What Constitutions Do*, New York: Oxford University Press.

—— (2002), *Risk and Reason: Safety, Law, and the Environment*, Cambridge: Cambridge University Press.

—— (2003), "Terrorism and Probability Neglect," *Journal of Risk and Uncertainty* 26(2–3): 121–136.

—— (2004a), "Moral Heuristics and Moral Framing," *Minnesota Law Review* 88: 1556–1597.

—— (2004b), "Response to Klein," *Econ Journal Watch* 1(2): 272–273.

—— (2005a), "Group Judgments: Statistical Means, Deliberation, and Information Markets," *New York University Law Review* 80(3): 962–1049.

—— (2005b), *Laws of Fear: Beyond the Precautionary Principle*, Cambridge: Cambridge University Press.

—— (2005c), *Radicals in Robes: Why Extreme Right-Wing Courts Are Wrong for America*, New York: Basic Books.

—— (2006), *Infotopia: How Many Minds Produce Knowledge*, New York: Oxford University Press.

—— (2009a), *Going to Extremes: How Like Minds Unite and Divide*, New York: Oxford University Press.

—— (2009b), *Worst Case Scenarios*, Cambridge, MA: Harvard University Press.

Sunstein, C. R., D. Kahneman, D. Schkade, and I. Ritov (2002), "Predictably Incoherent Judgments," *Stanford Law Review* 54(6): 1153–1215.

Sunstein, C. R., D. Schkade, and L. M. Ellman (2004), "Ideological Voting on Federal Courts of Appeals: A Preliminary Investigation," *Virginia Law Review* 90(1): 301–354.

Sunstein, C. R., D. Schkade, L. M. Ellman, and A. Sawicki (2006), *Are Judges Political? An Empirical Analysis of the Federal Judiciary*, Washington, DC: Brookings Institution Press.

Sunstein, C. R., and R. H. Thaler (2003a), "Libertarian Paternalism," *American Economic Review* 93(2): 175–179.

—— (2003b), "Libertarian Paternalism Is Not an Oxymoron," *University of Chicago Law Review* 70: 1159–1199.

———— (2008), *Nudge: Improving Decisions about Health, Wealth, and Happiness*, New Haven, CT: Yale University Press.

Sunstein, C. R., and E. Ullmann-Margalit (2000), "Second-Order Decisions," chap. 7 in *Behavioral Law and Economics*, Cambridge: Cambridge University Press.

Sunstein, C. R., and W. K. Viscusi (2002), *Punitive Damages: How Juries Decide*, Chicago: University of Chicago Press.

Takemura, K. (1994), "Influence of Elaboration on the Framing of Decision," *Journal of Psychology* 128: 33–39.

Talisse, R. B. (2009a), *Democracy and Moral Conflict*, Cambridge: Cambridge University Press.

———— (2009b), "Folk Epistemology and the Justification of Democracy," chap. 4 in *Does Truth Matter? Democracy and Public Space*, ed. R. Tinnevelt and R. Geenens, New York: Springer.

———— (2010), "An Epistemological Defense of Democracy," *Critical Review* 22 (2): 281–291.

Tetlock, P. E. (2005), *Expert Political Judgment: How Good Is It? How Can We Know?*, Princeton, NJ: Princeton University Press.

Thaler, R. H. (1991), *Quasi Rational Economics*, New York: Russell Sage Foundation.

———— (1992), *The Winner's Curse: Paradoxes and Anomalies of Economic Life*, Princeton, NJ: Princeton University Press.

———— (2000a), "From Homo Economicus to Homo Sapiens," *Journal of Economic Perspectives* 14(1): 133–141.

———— (2000b), "Mental Accounting Matters," in *Choices, Values, and Frames*, ed. D. Kahneman and A. Tversky, New York: Cambridge University Press.

———— (2000c), "Toward a Positive Theory of Consumer Choice," in *Choices, Values, and Frames*, ed. D. Kahneman and A. Tversky, New York: Cambridge University Press.

————, ed. (2005), *Advances in Behavioral Finance, Volume II*, Princeton, NJ: Princeton University Press.

Thaler, R. H., and C. R. Sunstein (2004), "Market Efficiency and Rationality: The Peculiar Case of Baseball," *Michigan Law Review* 102(6): 1390–1403.

Thaler, R. H., A. Tversky, D. Kahneman, and A. Schwartz (1997), "The Effect of Myopia and Loss Aversion on Risk Taking: An Experimental Test," *Quarterly Journal of Economics* 112(2): 647–661.

Trout, J. D. (2005), "Paternalism and Cognitive Bias," *Law and Philosophy* 24(4): 393–434.

———— (2009), *Why Empathy Matters: The Science and Psychology of Better Judgment*, New York: Penguin.

Tversky, A. (2000), "Rational Choice and the Framing of Decisions," in *Choices, Values, and Frames*, ed. D. Kahneman and A. Tversky, New York: Cambridge University Press.

Tversky, A., and D. Griffin (2000), "Endowments and Contrast in Judgments of Well-Being," in *Choices, Values, and Frames*, ed. D. Kahneman and A. Tversky, New York: Cambridge University Press.

Tversky, A., and D. Kahneman (1982), "Judgment under Uncertainty: Heuristics and Biases," in *Judgment under Uncertainty: Heuristics and Biases*, ed. D. Kahneman, P. Slovic, and A. Tversky, New York: Cambridge University Press.

——— (1983), "Extensional versus Intuitive Reasoning: The Conjunction Fallacy in Probability Judgment," *Psychological Review* 90(4): 293–315.

Tversky, A., and I. Simonson (2000), "Context-Dependent Preferences," in *Choices, Values, and Frames*, ed. D. Kahneman and A. Tversky, New York: Cambridge University Press.

Tversky, A., and R. H. Thaler (1990), "Anomalies: Preference Reversals," *Journal of Economic Perspectives* 4(2): 201–211.

van Aaken, A., C. List, and C. Luetge (2004), *Deliberation and Decision: Economics, Constitutional Theory and Deliberative Democracy*, Aldershot, UK: Ashgate.

Verhovek, S. H. (1997), "Houston Voters Maintain Affirmative-Action Policy," *New York Times*, November 6.

Viscusi, W. K. (1999), "How Do Judges Think about Risk?," *American Law and Economics Review* 1(1): 26–62.

——— (2001), "Jurors, Judges, and the Mistreatment of Risk by the Courts," *Journal of Legal Studies* 30(1): 107–142.

Viscusi, W. K., and R. J. Zeckhauser (2003), "Sacrificing Civil Liberties to Reduce Terrorism Risks," *Journal of Risk and Uncertainty* 26(2–3): 99–120.

Von Neumann, J., and O. Morgenstern (1944), *Theory of Games and Economic Behavior*, Princeton, NJ: Princeton University Press.

Wakker, P., and A. Tversky (1993), "An Axiomatization of Cumulative Prospect Theory," *Journal of Risk and Uncertainty* 7(2): 147–175.

Waldron, J. (1992), "The Irrelevance of Moral Objectivity," in *Natural Law Theory: Contemporary Essays*, ed. R. George, New York: Oxford University Press.

——— (1993a), "A Right-Based Critique of Constitutional Rights," *Oxford Journal of Legal Studies* 13(1): 18–51.

——— (1993b), "Rights and Majorities: Rousseau Revisited," in *Liberal Rights: Collected Papers, 1981–1991*, ed. J. Waldron, Cambridge: Cambridge University Press.

——— (1998a), "Judicial Review and the Conditions of Democracy," *Journal of Political Philosophy* 6(4): 335–355.

——— (1998b), "Moral Truth and Judicial Review," *American Journal of Jurisprudence* 43: 75–97.

——— (1998c), "Precommitment and Disagreement," in *Constitutionalism: Philosophical Foundations*, ed. L. Alexander, Cambridge: Cambridge University Press.

——— (1999a), "Deliberation, Disagreement and Voting," in *Deliberative Democracy and Human Rights*, ed. H. Koh and R. Slye, New Haven, CT: Yale University Press.

——— (1999b), *The Dignity of Legislation*, Cambridge: Cambridge University Press.

——— (1999c), *Law and Disagreement*, Oxford: Oxford University Press.

——— (2002), "Judicial Power and Popular Sovereignty," in *Marbury versus Madison: Documents and Commentary*, ed. M. Graber and M. Perhac, Washington, DC: CQ Press.

—— (2004a), "Judicial Review and Republican Government," in *That Eminent Tribunal: Judicial Supremacy and the Constitution*, ed. C. Wolfe, Princeton, NJ: Princeton University Press.

—— (2004b), "Some Models of Dialogue between Judges and Legislators," *Supreme Court Law Review* 23(2d): 7–47.

—— (2006), "The Core of the Case against Judicial Review," *Yale Law Journal* 115(6): 1346–1407.

Weinstein, N. D., and W. M. Klein (2002), "Resistance of Personal Risk Perceptions to Debiasing Interventions," in *Heuristics and Biases: The Psychology of Intuitive Judgment*, ed. T. Gilovich, D. Griffin, and D. Kahneman, New York: Cambridge University Press.

Weirich, P. (1986), "Rousseau on Proportional Majority Rule," *Philosophy and Phenomenological Research* 47(1): 111–126.

Wills, C. E. (1999), "On the Role of Framing Effects in Assessment of Health-Related Utilities," *Medical Decision Making* 19(4): 505–506.

Wolff, R. P. (1998), *In Defense of Anarchism*, Berkeley: University of California Press.

Woodside, A. G., and C. Dubelaar (2003), "Increasing Quality in Measuring Advertising Effectiveness: A Meta-analysis of Question Framing in Conversion Studies," *Journal of Advertising Research* 43(1): 78–85.

Zagzebski, L. T. (1996), *Virtues of the Mind: An Inquiry into the Nature of Virtue and the Ethical Foundations of Knowledge*, Cambridge: Cambridge University Press.

—— (2003), "Intellectual Motivation and the Good of Truth," in *Intellectual Virtue: Perspectives from Ethics and Epistemology*, ed. M. DePaul and L. T. Zagzebski, Oxford: Oxford University Press.

Zaller, J. R. (1992), *The Nature and Origins of Mass Opinion*, Cambridge: Cambridge University Press.

Zuckerman, A. (1977), "The Concept 'Political Elite': Lessons from Mosca and Pareto," *Journal of Politics* 39(2): 324–344.

Index